Jon Tobe

W9-CAP-817

# The Book of
# Genesis

# The Book of Genesis

## An Exposition by
## Charles R. Erdman

**BAKER BOOK HOUSE**
Grand Rapids, Michigan 49506

Copyright 1950 by
Fleming H. Revell Company
Paperback edition issued 1982 by
Baker Book House
with permission of copyright owner

ISBN: 0-8010-3375-6

PHOTOLITHOPRINTED BY CUSHING - MALLOY, INC.
ANN ARBOR, MICHIGAN, UNITED STATES OF AMERICA

*"In the beginning God"*

# *Introduction*

THE BOOK OF GENESIS IS MUCH MORE THAN A FASCInating collection of short stories. It is this, and indeed to these stories, with their dramatic movement and intense human interest, a high place has been assigned in the literature of the world.

However, this is a book of history and its narratives are of such importance that without them it would be difficult to understand the Scriptures of the Old and New Testaments. These narratives are records of unique and initial events, of beginnings and origins, so that the book is properly named *Genesis*, which is a Greek word meaning "origin." The book opens with the story of creation (1:1 to 2:3). This is followed by a sketch of human history down to the birth of Abraham (2:4 to 11:26). The remaining and main portion of the book presents the lives of the four patriarchs from whose family came the people of Israel and ultimately the Saviour of the world.

The author of Genesis arranges his literary material in ten sections, each marked by the formula: "These are the generations of." The first concerns "the generations of the heavens and the earth," and is introductory to the sections which follow and which begin the histories of the different families of man, particularly of the people of Israel. It may be of interest to note the connections in which this formula is used:

"The generations of the heavens and the earth" (2:4); "the book of the generations of Adam" (5:1); "the generations of Noah" (6:9); "the generations of the sons of Noah" (10:1); "the generations of Shem" (11:10), "of Terah" (11:27), "of Ishmael" (25:12), "of Isaac" (25:19), "of Esau" (36:1,9), "of Jacob" (37:2). Such an analysis shows that from a literary point of view the book of Genesis was arranged carefully, even elaborately, and with a distinct unity of purpose.

However, the supreme value of the book is not literary or historical, but religious. Here is the revelation of one God, infinitely powerful, wise and good, and an account of His relation to the origin of the world and to the history of nations. Here are recorded the beginnings of life, of sin, of apostasy, of punishment, of atonement, of worship, of prophecy and of salvation. Genesis forms the first chapter in the history of redemption, which is the substance of the entire Bible. It points forward from a Paradise Lost to a Paradise Regained.

The moral and spiritual instruction of the book is the more impressive, and is of immediate application to personal problems of the present day, from the fact that it is presented, not in precepts or in philosophic theories, but in the form of biographies. Here are found not mythical heroes but actual men with whom God had definite dealings, to whom He showed His mercy and grace, and through whom He promised to bring blessing to the whole world.

Some of the religious values of the book may be emphasized by dividing its contents into the biographies of its seven chief characters. These might be treated as typical and might symbolize seven aspects of the life of man in his relation to God and as redeemed by grace. Such a division may form an index to the book and may summarize something of its spiritual message: I. Adam: *Man*, created, fallen, redeemed, Chs. 1-3; II. Enoch: *The New Nature*, Chs. 4, 5; III; Noah: *Resurrection*, Chs. 6:1-11:26; IV. Abraham: *Faith*, Chs. 11:27-25:10; V. Isaac: *Sonship*, Chs. 25:11-28:5 and 35:21-29; VI. Jacob: *Discipline and Service*, Chs. 25:19-50:13; VII. Joseph: *Sovereignty*, Chs. 37-50.

# Contents

*The Book of Genesis*

# I

## ADAM

GENESIS 1 TO 3

THE TERM "ADAM" MAY DESIGNATE AN INDIVIDUAL OR indicate the race of mankind. In Genesis, the narratives connected with the term are so significant, so symbolic, so prophetic, as to throw a flood of light on the origin, the character and the destiny of man.

First of all, then, man is a *created being*, and of the creation he is the climax, the glory, and the crown. The account of his origin forms a part of the story which includes the first chapter of Genesis. The whole story is one of majesty and beauty. It is composed with such symmetry, such rhythm, such evident design as to constitute a superb poem. It may be regarded as the sublime Epic of Creation (Genesis 1:1-2:3).

The contents include a comprehensive introduction (verses 1 and 2), a dramatic movement, covering six creative "days" (verses 3 to 31), and a triumphant conclusion, the Sabbath of God (Ch. 2:1-3). The "introduction" records the origin of the universe, its primitive state, and the power by which it was brought to perfection. At whatever time, and by whatever process, it was God by whom "the heaven and the earth" were created. The original character of this creation was "without form and void." It was "desolateness and emptiness" and was shrouded in darkness. Yet God was present. His Spirit, His "breath," brooded over the vast chaos, ready and able to impart order and beauty and life (verses 1, 2).

The six days are divided into two symmetrical series of three days each. The first series is concerned with the physical world, and may be regarded as the era of matter; the second series relates the creation of organized beings, of animals and man, and is the era of life. Each series begins with light, the first with cosmic light, the second with the light of the sun. In both series the third day includes two creative works, while to each of the other days is assigned but one. Each of the six days begins with an "evening" which develops into a "morning." The concluding day records the "rest" of the Creator.

"And God said, Let there be light; and there was light" (verses 3-5). Such is the impressive record of the first act in the divine drama. It is supposed that the light was produced by imparting movement to the vast, inert mass of created matter. Of that process nothing is said, but it is recorded that "God divided the light from the darkness" and "God called the light day and the darkness he called night." This devleopment from chaotic darkness to cosmic light is designated as an "evening" and a "morning."

"And God saw the light that it was good." Indeed, light may be regarded as the most beautiful, the most beneficent, the loveliest feature of the physical world. It is a symbol of God Himself, for "God is light," and He has revealed His glory "in the face of Jesus Christ"

(II Cor. 4:6), who is the "light of the world" (John 9:5).

It is recorded that on the "second day" "God made the firmament." This word is an unfortunate translation. It is from a Latin term which indicates something "firm" or "solid." On the contrary, the Hebrew word means a vast "expanse." It does not denote the metallic dome which the ancients supposed overarched the earth; nor does it define the sky or the atmosphere surrounding our globe, as many moderns imagine. It indicates the measureless "expanse" of the "heavens," with all their innumerable starry hosts. On the first day, it seems the motion of matter brought light; on the second day matter was organized into an ordered universe (verses 6-8).

The "third day" fixes the thought on our planet. The dry land appears, separated from the seas, and a new element is introduced in the form of vegetation. This is not sentient life. It belongs to the sphere of matter. Its story is a preface to the record of the appearance of animal life. The plant did not develop out of the minerals on which it lives. From these it is distinct. Nor did it develop into animal life, which it supports. Nor need it be supposed that on this third day vegetation appeared in all the higher forms which are named. It seems to be the method of the writer to mention an order of facts but once, and this at the time of its introduction. He records the ultimate as well as the immediate results of an act. Plant life appeared on the "third day"; many of its forms could not have existed until after the appearance of the sun. It was, however, the harbinger of a nobler time to come. It was the link between the age of matter and the age of animals and of man (verses 9-13).

It is not necessary to believe that the sun and the moon came into existence in the period of time indicated by the "fourth day." It is understood commonly that when the "luminous envelope" which surrounded the globe was dispelled, the sun and moon and stars appeared. The heavenly bodies then fulfilled their appointed purpose. They were the "luminaries" to mark day and night and seasons and years, and to produce those conditions necessary for the existence of living beings on the earth (verses 14-19).

Between the life of plants and of animals there is a mysterious but impassable gulf. This is indicated by assigning the origin of animal life to a separate day. This "fifth day" records the creation of the lower animals, in the water and the air. The distinction from vegetation is further emphasized by the use of the significant word for "create" (Hebrew, bara), which is used of the original creation of matter (verse 1), and a third time of the creation of man (verse 27), and is understood to indicate a direct exercise of divine creative power.

Objection has been brought to the narrative on the ground that mention is made of "whales" among these lower animals instead of among the mammals mentioned in the following day. However, the original word does not indicate "whales" but is a picturesque term which may be translated "great stretched-out sea monsters," describing creatures properly belonging to this age of reptiles and fowls (verses 20-23).

Of the "sixth day" the two recorded works are the creation of the higher animals, and the creation of man. That these are assigned to the same age accords with the fact that the physical nature of man is closely related to that of the animal. That his spiritual nature is akin to God is emphasized by the mention of the divine purpose: "Let us make man in our image, after our likeness." So, in a later verse, it is stated, "The Lord God formed man of the dust of the ground and breathed into his nostrils the breath of life" (2:7). The "dust of the ground" may mean the common elements of matter, but exactly what its form, or its previous character, or what its possible relation to the animal, it is useless to conjecture. Nothing is indicated as to the time or the process of this creation. By the "image" and "likeness of God" is indicated the mental and moral nature of man, his powers of reason and intelligence, his free will and self-consciousness, and his capacity for communion with God.

These characteristics distinguished man from the lower creatures and inevitably insured that dominion over them which God ordained. The vegetation already provided was to be the staple food to supply the physical needs of man and beast; but fellowship with God was made possible by the spiritual nature imparted to man (verses 24-30).

Special provision for such fellowship was made by the example and ordinance of God, when "on the seventh day God ended his work which he had made; and he rested on the seventh day." The work of creation was complete. It had reached its climax in the creation of man. The elements brought into existence were indestructible, the laws established are unchanging. Yet the "rest of God" does not denote inaction. His work of creation ended but He did not abandon His creation. His work of providence was to continue; His work of redemption would soon be begun (see John 5:17). Likewise, his labor would be assigned to man, but there would be provided for him periods of rest. Above all, there would be one day in seven, "blessed" and "sanctified," when his body could be refreshed and his soul "restored" by worship and by fellowship with his Creator and his Redeemer (2:1-3).

Thus the inspired Epic of Creation comes to its close. The author has shown remarkable modesty and restraint. While he does not anticipate the details of modern science, his noble lines are in harmony with established facts.

"It is one of the more than human qualities of the language of the Holy Scriptures that, while written by men whose knowledge was in accordance with their times, it does not contradict the increased knowledge of later times." *

The "days of creation" were not measured by the sun; three had ended before the sun appeared; one comprehended all the possibly vast ages during which "the heavens and the earth" came to their present state (2:4). No process or method of creation is proposed. There is an orderly progress from lower to higher, from matter to life, and from lower beings to man; yet life does not develop from matter, nor does the animal develop into man. Each of the three great

* *Bible Commentary* edited by Bishop Charles J. Ellicott, "Genesis," p. 11.

steps in creation is attributed to a specific action of
the divine will.

The purpose of the inspired composer is to reveal
the origin of man, and to present him as the crowning
act of a wise and powerful and loving Creator. Thus
he rebukes the atheist who says in his folly, "There is
no God." He enlightens the polytheist who worships
many gods. He refutes the pantheist who identifies
God with what God has created. He convicts the
materialist of childish credulity in believing that the
universe is the product of chance, and that "everything
was created by no one out of nothing." "God created
man in his own image" (1:27) is the most rational
explanation of the origin and nature of man.

As the Hymn of Creation ends, the first chapter of
human history begins (2:4-25). The earth has been
prepared for the habitation of man. His origin is
again mentioned (2:7), not here as the climax of a
process but as the beginning of a career. He is placed
in a garden "eastward in Eden." To him is assigned
the task of caring for its fruits and its flowers. Among
its beautiful trees stands the mysterious "tree of life,"
and also the "tree of good and evil," from which man
is forbidden to eat. With the many living creatures
Adam becomes familiar and gives to them appropriate
and descriptive names. For him a fit companion is
provided, woman, taken from his side, the last and
most perfect work of the Creator.

The language is figurative, but contains the record
of facts, and conveys messages of supreme importance.
Man is presented once more as both a physical and
a spiritual being. "God formed him from the dust

of the ground and breathed into his nostrils the breath
of life" (verse 7). His superior powers of intellect
and reason are shown in his study of the birds and
beasts and in his ability to attribute to each one its
proper character. The dignity of labor is indicated by
the fact that even in paradise a task is assigned to
occupy the faculties of man. The supreme message is
contained in relating the creation of woman. Made
not simply "from the dust of the ground," but taken
from the side of man, molded and fashioned to be his
equal and counterpart, she is presented to Adam as
his "other self," and the inspired writer adds the
divine injunction quoted by our Lord: "Therefore
shall a man leave his father and his mother, and shall
cleave unto his wife; and they shall be one flesh."
Thus the ordinance of marriage was established and
sanctified. Thus the blessedness of man was made
complete (2:4-25).

Man is a created being, but he is also a *fallen being,*
and in the story of his fall every human soul can find
some echo of its own experience. The temptation
came in the form of a "serpent," but most readers
see in that serpent a symbol or an instrument of "that
old serpent, called the Devil, and Satan, which de-
ceiveth the whole world" (Rev. 12:9). The whole
story is symbolic and figurative, yet its symbols and
figures relate actual events and convey vital truths
which are not difficult to discern. Temptation is in
itself like a serpent, "subtle," treacherous, silent in
its approach, appearing when least expected, able to
fascinate its victim, swift, venomous in its attack,
deadly in its power. The tempter began by raising

questions as to the wisdom and justice and love of God. This is the most insidious method of attacking the human soul. Surprise is feigned that God has placed any restriction on man. "Yea, hath God said, Ye shall not eat of every tree of the garden." This was an exaggeration; it implied that God unwisely had limited the actions of His creatures. He had denied them the enjoyment of the delicious fruit in which the garden abounded. It is the familiar suggestion of Satan that to obey God is to take out of life all its richness and possible happiness and joy.

The woman makes the truthful reply: "We may eat of the fruit of the trees of the garden; but of the fruit of the tree which is in the midst of the garden, God hath said, Ye shall not eat of it, neither shall ye touch it, lest ye die." That is to say, life is full of enjoyments and blessings and innocent pleasures. There are countless trees offering us their rich fruit. Yet there are some things which are wrong. God knows that the fruit of some trees is deadly poison to the soul. In His wisdom He warns us to avoid what some trees offer.

To this wise answer, and to the solemn warning it repeats, the tempter makes his impious reply. He flatly contradicts the word of God. He dares to say: "Ye shall not surely die." Today he is saying to us: "You can sin without suffering. It is quite safe to break the laws of God. Do not believe that 'whatsoever a man soweth that shall he also reap.' It is an exploded myth that 'the wages of sin is death.'"

Then the tempter ventures even further and declares that to disobey God not only will involve no penalty but will result in the very highest good. The thing which God forbids is the very thing we need. He does not love us. He is even jealous of us, and knows that we would be almost divine if we should always do exactly as we please. As to this "tree of knowledge," or as to tasting every wrong and forbidden pleasure, "God doth know that in the day ye eat thereof, then your eyes shall be opened, and ye shall be as gods, knowing good and evil."

When doubt had entered, when the defense provided by faith in God had been broken down, then the temptation was presented in all its irresistible power: "The woman saw that the tree was good for food, and that it was pleasant to the eyes, and a tree to be desired to make one wise." Here was an appeal to fleshly appetite, and an appeal to ambition, and an appeal to curiosity. There are no new temptations. All the assaults of the tempter are but forms and variations of these three. So Christ was tempted (Matt. 4:1-11). Thus John summarizes "all that is in the world" which makes us turn from God, "the lust of the flesh, the lust of the eyes and the pride of life" (I John 2:16).

Possibly to the woman "curiosity" made the strongest appeal. She wanted to see what the result would be. She was not desirous of evil but wished to learn by experience something which God had forbidden her to know. At least, we all realize the appeal of curiosity, and the desire "to see what it would be like" to be free from restraints; possibly to be so wise, so sophisticated, so independent, that we can do without God; and to secure such imagined benefits we venture to disobey His laws.

So it was with the woman. Venturing near the tree, "she took of the fruit thereof and did eat, and gave also unto her husband with her; and he did eat." In offering the fruit to Adam she was not moved by malice, that he might be involved in her guilt. She had a loving desire that he might participate in her expected enjoyment. As for Adam, he was not deceived as Eve had been (I Tim. 2:14). In accepting what she offered he wished to show his affection and his willingness to share her fate. However, the most passionate love does not make it right to do what one believes to be wrong. Both acted freely; both knew that they were breaking the law of God; both were guilty of sin; for in the gift of freedom had been involved moral responsibility. They might have chosen to obey God. They chose to disobey; and what is sin but transgression of law?

What, then, was the result? First of all, it was shame: "The eyes of both of them were opened, and they knew that they were naked." They had gained knowledge but they had lost innocence. There was mental growth but moral loss. Conscience had been awakened and they know the sense of guilt. They wished to hide from one another and from themselves. It is a pitiful experience for one to lose self-respect.

More desperately still, they wished to hide from God. The first result of sin was shame, and the second was fear. They had enjoyed fellowship with God. Now they stood in dread of Him. "They heard the voice of the Lord God walking in the garden in the

cool of the day; and Adam and his wife hid themselves from the presence of the Lord God amongst the
trees of the garden." It was in "the cool of the day";
so when passion has calmed and the time of reflection
has come, fear of God and the consciousness of sin
torment the soul. In that sense, too, "conscience
makes cowards of us all."

It was childish to seek to hide from God "amongst
the trees of the garden"; it is much more foolish to
try to conceal guilt by flimsy excuses which shift on
others the fault which is our own. When "in the cool
of day" we realize that God knows where one is and
what one has done, it is the part of wisdom to repent, to confess, and to beg for the mercy of God;
but the man attempted to put all the blame on the
woman and even on God: "And the man said, The
woman whom thou gavest to be with me, she gave
me of the tree and I did eat." Then the woman attempted to shift the blame on the tempter, "And the
woman said, The serpent beguiled me and I did eat."
The attempt to conceal our sin by attributing the
fault to others is as futile as to seek to escape from
God by hiding among the trees.

The first consequence of sin was shame; the second
was fear; the third was the sentence of penalty and
doom. For the serpent it was to be a loathsome life
and ultimately a fatal wound. For the woman it was
to be pain and sorrow, and subjection to man. For
the man it was to be toil and bitter struggle, decay and
death. Indeed, the penalty is at once inflicted, for
the essence of death is not merely the separation of
soul and body, but the separation of the soul from

God. This, sin already had accomplished. Man's fellowship with God had ended, and lest he might eat of the tree of life and so escape physical death, he is driven out from Eden, and cherubim with a flaming sword are stationed to prevent his return to the garden. His condition is desperate. "By one man sin entered into the world and by sin death."

However, man is not only a created and a fallen being; man has been *redeemed*. The first faint prophecy of this redemption is included in the very phrases of the curse pronounced on the serpent: "I will put enmity between thee and the woman, and between thy seed and her seed; it shall bruise thy head, and thou shalt bruise his heel." Surely this is the language of allegory; but it conveys sublime truth. There is more intended here than a literal reference to the foot of a man and the sting of a serpent. Those readers seem justified who regard this sentence as the "protevangelium," or the "first proclamation of the Gospel," predicting the final triumph of Christ over Satan and sin. From this fountainhead the prophecy of redemption widens in an ever-broadening stream. This is the one theme of Scripture. There would ever be a conflict between man and the "serpent," but complete victory over evil would ultimately be attained by One, the Seed of the woman, in whom this word of hope would be fulfilled. Yet this victory could be attained only through suffering. The very "coats of skin" mentioned in the story involved the sacrifice of life. One who was "wounded for our transgression" would provide for each of us a robe of righteousness.

Adam heard the word of promise, and, believing, he

was delivered from despair. So it would seem. He called his wife "Eve" ("Life") "because she was the mother of all living." Her Seed would at last conquer death, and those who would truly trust in Him would inherit eternal life. Unaided, man could not overcome the tempter nor regain an entrance into Eden; but a Redeemer would appear who would make it possible for His followers to "bruise Satan" under their feet (Romans 16:20), and would fling open wide for them the gates of the Garden and give them "to eat of the tree of life, which is in the midst of the paradise of God" (Rev. 2:7).

# II

## *ENOCH*

FROM ADAM TWO LINES OF DESCENDANTS ARE TRACED, one through his eldest son, Cain, another through a younger son, Seth. The first line, as illustrated by Cain and Lamech, indicates how the nature of man has been impaired and corrupted by disobedience to God. The second, exemplified by *Enoch*, shows that by faith a *new nature* is imparted to men whereby fellowship with God can be enjoyed.

How far man had fallen from "righteousness and true holiness" is demonstrated by the cruel and impious character of Cain. The sin of Adam had consisted in disobedience to God; the career of Cain, his son, showed utter disregard and defiance of God. In striking contrast to his brother, Abel was pre-eminently a man of faith. This faith was revealed in his conduct. While "the works" of Cain "were evil," his "brother's" were "righteous." His faith was shown also in the way in which he worshiped God. "Cain brought of the fruit of the ground an offering unto the Lord. And Abel, he also brought of the firstlings of his flock and of the fat thereof. And the Lord had respect unto Abel and to his offering: but unto Cain and to his offering he had not respect" (Ch. 4:3-5).

The offering of Abel was accepted because he came in faith, with a heart of penitence, of trust, of devotion. The worship of Cain was a mere formal act, expressing no real submission or love.

The writer of "Hebrews" seems to indicate that the very form of his offering was due to the faith of Abel. He is mentioned by the writer as the first in a long list of heroes who lived "by faith." In this connection, the term "faith" appears to indicate the motive of men who believed what God had said and who acted on that belief. If this is what is meant by the "faith" of Abel, then God must have revealed to him in some way that the proper approach to God was by the offering of a life. "By faith Abel offered unto God a more excellent sacrifice than Cain, by which he obtained witness that he was righteous, God testifying of his gifts; and by it he being dead yet speaketh" (Heb. 11:4).

This offering of a lamb, may indicate, even if in type and symbol, the provision which God has made for sinful man to receive pardon and to enjoy fellowship with Him. It may remind us that there is no other way, and that without shedding of blood there is no remission of sin. The sacrifice outside the gate of Eden may point us forward to the "Lamb of God that taketh away the sin of the world" (John 1:29), or upward to the heavenly choirs which are chanting the song of adoration "worthy the Lamb that was slain to receive power and riches, and wisdom, and strength, and honor, and glory, and blessing" (Rev. 5:12).

Undoubtedly God did recognize the difference

which faith and unbelief wrought in the lives and in the worship of the two men. The story of Cain is tragic. An act of worship and its issue were the occasion of his crime, and it is pitiful to recall how often religious observances and forms have divided men and been the causes of hatred and cruelty and bitter strife.

When his offering was not accepted, "Cain was very wroth and his countenance fell." God saw the deadly jealousy which embittered him, and he remonstrated with Cain and warned him of the evil which might come from his ungoverned envy and temper. Yet Cain "rose up against Abel his brother and slew him." When faced with his crime he denied his guilt, and insolently disavowed any responsibility for his brother. He is told that the blood of his brother is crying for vengeance. The author of Hebrews reminds us that "the blood of Jesus speaketh better things than that of Abel" (Heb. 12:24). The voice of the one cried for punishment and retribution; the other speaks of reconciliation and of peace.

Upon Cain judgment is pronounced. He is driven out from the lands he has been cultivating and becomes a fugitive and a wanderer. He expresses no penitence, only fear of death. God spares him and graciously gives him a token that his life is not to be taken from him in vengeance.

Cain goes eastward and ultimately builds a city, and his descendants become the founders of a civilization, great but godless. The most prominent of this family of Cain was *Lamech*. He was a bigamist and a murderer; yet one of his sons was the originator of commercial life, amassing property in cattle; another son, Jubal, was the inventor of harps and organs, and is properly regarded as the "father" of the fine arts; a third son, Tubal-cain, became "an instructor of every artificer in brass and iron," the forerunner or founder of all mechanical and scientific arts and inventions. The daughter of Lamech was noted for her charm and beauty. Lamech himself was a poet; yet in his cruel song he defends himself for the murder of which he boasts to his two wives, and expresses an arrogant confidence that, with the weapons of brass and iron provided by his son, his death would be avenged, not only sevenfold, as promised to Cain, but seventy and sevenfold.

His proud insolent verses have been translated as follows:

> Adah and Zillah, hear my voice;
> Ye wives of Lamech, give ear unto my rede,
> For I have slain a man for wounding me:
> Even a young man for bruising me.
> Truly Cain shall be avenged sevenfold,
> And Lamech seventy and sevenfold.

With this proud poem, with its boast of bigamy and bloodshed, the history of the line of Cain comes to its close. This race, with all its glory and achievement and culture and progress, was to be swept away, and the race of mankind preserved through the godly remnant found in the family of Noah.

This history is not without its warning for the present age. Our own civilization is on trial. Its material and scientific and cultural progress has not been accompanied by an equal advance in morality, in spiritual development, and in religious conviction. It is well for us to be warned, and a note of admonition is sounded in the fate of this brilliant early civilization which, because of its godlessness, perished in the flood.

The record of the descendants of Cain is in striking contrast with the story of the line of Seth and Enoch and Noah which follows (Ch. 5). These men had no achievements in art or culture or invention of which to boast. The account of their lives is rather drab and monotonous. To each one is attributed a large number of years; each "begat sons and daughters," and "died." All died, except one. His name is that of the most notable character between Adam and Noah. He lived on earth fewer years than any of his family, and he never died. "By faith Enoch was translated, that he should not see death, and was not found because God has translated him" (Heb. 11:5). Yet the way in which Enoch left the world is hardly less remakable than the way in which, for more than three hundred years, he had lived in the world. In a brief biography of less than ten lines it is twice recorded that "Enoch walked with God." In the Epistle to the Hebrews a parallel phrase is used, "He pleased God."

This is the surprising fact. Here was a son of Adam, here was a man who had inherited a nature impaired by sin and predisposed to evil, here was a man in whose veins flowed the same blood as that of murderers like Cain and Lamech, yet this man "walked with God."

It must be evident that the ability to walk with God, or to please God, is not due to any inherited goodness or virtue. Some of Enoch's ancestors had been worshipers of God; noble traditions or virtues and admirable traits of character may pass from one generation to another, and influences of family and friends may have their effect, but no man, by nature, is fit for fellowship with God, or can walk so as to be well pleasing to God. However, by faith a *new nature* is imparted; one receives a spiritual rebirth, and of such a new nature Enoch affords an example and a type.

It should also be noted that walking with God does not denote a life of solitude, or necessitate withdrawing from our fellow men. Enoch was apparently a man of affairs. He was a busy man in a world of busy men. His occupation was that of a farmer, and that in a time when agriculture had become very difficult, and men were hoping that God would remove the curse from the soil, so that the earth might bring forth more abundantly. Under such conditions, it seems, Enoch found it necessary to toil incessantly for the support of a large family. Yet such domestic and humble tasks are fit instruments for the development of a godly life. Enoch was certainly no recluse, but was known in his own community; for we read that when he was translated "he could not be found," which may indicate that, as in the similar case of Elijah, he was missed and a search was made for him.

Nor does walking with God depend on sinless surroundings. It may be easier so to walk when enjoying the "fellowship of saints"; Enoch did have the companionship of godly relatives. Yet he lived in evil days. Wickedness and corruption were becoming worse and worse. However, in those days "Enoch

walked with God." The very life of a good man will
be a rebuke to the godless. He may arouse their envy
and their enmity. It may even be the duty of a righteous man to warn others of the certain punishment of
sin. Such was the supreme task of Enoch. He predicted the coming judgment of God. His message is
recorded in the Epistle of Jude. When the writer has
described the depravity, the insolence, the hypocrisy
of the men of his own day, he declares that to men of
this same kind Enoch had brought his announcement
of doom.

"And Enoch also, the seventh from Adam, proph-
esied to these saying, Behold, the Lord cometh with
ten thousands of his holy ones to execute judgment
upon all, and to convict all that are ungodly among
them of all their ungodly deeds which they have ungodly committed, and of all their hard speeches which
ungodly sinners have spoken against him" (Jude 14,
15).

Enoch was the "seventh from Adam," descended in
the godly line of Seth. Lamech was the "seventh
from Adam," descended from the apostate Cain. Contrast the wild "Hymn of Hate" composed by the murderer and bigamist Lamech with this solemn *Dies Irae*
which came from the lips of the man who walked with
God.

What made the difference between the two men
and their messages? Both were sons of Adam. Both
had inherited a fallen nature; but to Enoch a new
nature was imparted through the instrument of faith.
It was by faith that he was able to please God. "But
without faith it is impossible to please him; for he

that cometh to God must believe that he is, and that he is a rewarder of them that diligently seek him" (Heb. 11:6).

What is faith? It is "taking God at his word" and acting on that belief. Just how God had spoken to Enoch and revealed His presence, His pardoning grace, His future purpose, we do not know; but Enoch's life was a response to such messages of mercy. By faith he "walked with God," he had fellowship with God, he pleased God, he bore witness for God.

To men in all the ages the same experiences have been possible. We find the supreme revelation of God in his Son our Saviour, the Lord Jesus Christ. By believing in Him we have peace with God, we become true "children of God," we have fellowship with God, and we "rejoice in hope of the glory of God."

Such glory is the certain issue of a life of faith. "Enoch walked with God and he was not, for God took him" (Gen. 5:24). Suddenly, without pain or death, he was transported into the visible presence of the Lord, with whom, unseen, he had been walking through the years.

As one has said, "Enoch walked with God and one day he walked so far that he never came back again." Another has remarked that "Enoch walked on the heights and he simply stepped off into heaven."

Such a departure has been taken as a description of death, and, indeed, it may be used as a figure of that mysterious experience by which one is enabled "to depart and to be with Christ."

However, Enoch did not die: "By faith Enoch was translated that he should not see death; and was not found because God translated him." Such was the experience of Elijah, who went up by a whirlwind into heaven. So, too, our Lord was walking with His disciples when "he was taken up, and a cloud received him out of their sight." Such, too, is the blessed hope of His followers, who look for His appearing, and long for a reunion with those who have gone before to be with their Saviour. "We which are alive and remain unto the coming of the Lord . . . shall be caught up together with them in the clouds, to meet the Lord in the air: and so shall we ever be with the Lord. Wherefore comfort one another with these words" (I Thess. 4:15-18).

# III

## *NOAH*

IT IS NATURAL AND RIGHT TO ASSOCIATE NOAH WITH
the flood, which has become a historic symbol of
doom and destruction and death; yet there is another
side to the story. Noah is also a type and symbol of
*resurrection*, of revival and of renewed life.

His very name means "comfort" or "rest." It was
given him by his father as an expression of hope: "He
called his name Noah, saying, This same shall comfort us for all our work and for the toil of our hands,
because of the ground which the Lord hath cursed."

Noah, indeed, was to be the father of a new race.
In him a new world was to begin. Yet it was to be
life from the dead. "Rest" and "comfort" could come
only when judgment had fallen and the old world had
been swept away.

Of such judgment there was appalling need. The
universal corruption of the race is recorded in the
most arresting terms: "God saw that the wickedness
of man was great in the earth, and that every imagination of the thoughts of his heart was only evil
continually" (Ch. 6:5). This indictment is more
severe and more impressive than could have been
made by any list of revolting crimes. It traces the ab-

38

normal wickedness to its real source, namely, to the unbridled imagination, to the corrupt thoughts and the impure desires of the human heart.

The reason assigned for the increasing moral degradation was the marriages of the "sons of God" with the "fair" and enticing "daughters of men." This probably means that there were intermarriages between the godly line of Seth and the godless descendants of Cain. The result, as usual, was not the elevation of the lower to the higher level of life, but the dragging down of the godly to the character and ideals and practices of the godless and profane.

In those days there were "giants," or possibly "tyrants ruling by force." As a result of the abnormal marriages, men of fierce and warlike character filled the earth with violence. The universal corruption of the race was thus characterized by reckless sensuality and heartless cruelty.

In notable contrast with this universal degradation was the character of Noah. He is described as "a just man and perfect in his generation"; and it is stated, as in the case of Enoch, that he "walked with God." Thus his life was one of purity and piety, passed in constant and habitual companionship with God, in harmony with the purposes of God and submissive to His will. To him God revealed His sorrow over the sins of the world and the necessity of purifying judgment. He also promised a long period of respite during which there might be time for repentance (Ch. 6:3).

The character of Noah and his deliverance from impending doom are traced to their source in the free and unmerited favor of God: "Noah found grace in the eyes of the Lord" (verse 8). On the human side, however, there was the instrument of faith. Noah was a man who believed what God had revealed, and acted on that belief. "By the faith of Noah, being warned of God concerning things not seen as yet, moved with godly fear, prepared an ark to the saving of his house; through which he condemned the world, and became the heir of the righteousness which is according to faith" (Heb. 11:7).

Noah showed his faith by pleading with his fellow men to repent and by warning them of their approaching doom. He is called a "preacher of righteousness" (II Peter 2:5). Still more surprisingly was his faith exhibited by his building the ark. In the judgment of his acquaintances hardly a more absurd and fantastic procedure could have been conceived. There, far inland, distant from the ocean, with no water in sight, he worked, day after day, constructing a great vessel fitted to float on stormy seas. The dimensions of the strange craft were divinely appointed, as also were the accommodations necessary for Noah and his family, and also for animals in pairs which were to be saved for the preservation of the species. When all was in readiness Noah was shut in the ark, and the dread visitation began. For forty days and forty nights there was a devastating downpour of rain, until the rivers and also the sea burst their boundaries, or, in the picturesque language of the story, "the fountains of the great deep were broken up, and the windows [or "flood-gates"] of heaven were opened." Some readers conclude that a convulsion of nature set loose some vast volume of water. Probably the whole description is in the terms of eyewitnesses. The tradition vividly sets forth the catastrophe as viewd by Noah and his family, when it declares that "all the high hills that were under the whole heaven were covered." It is not necessary even to believe that the flood covered the whole globe. The disaster certainly was universal so far as the human race was concerned. The historic truth is attested by the fact that among all nations there remain traditions of a flood which destroyed all mankind except one family. It is quite enough to believe the inspired narrative that "all flesh died that moved upon the earth," and that "every living substance was destroyed . . . from the earth; and Noah only remained alive, and they that were with him in the ark" (Ch. 7:23).

As to those who perished in this dire catastrophe, our Saviour refers to them in warning His own followers. Of their monstrous sins He makes no mention. He notes only their careless indifference and unbelief. They were engaged in their usual pursuits, which were in themselves innocent, but to be so immersed in these as to forget or to despise the messenger of God was foolish and fatal. "But as the days of Noah were, so shall also the coming of the Son of man be. For as in the days that were before the flood they were eating and drinking, marrying and giving in marriage, until the day that Noah entered into the ark, and knew not until the flood came, and took them all away; so also shall the coming of the Son of man be. . . . Watch therefore: for ye know not what hour your Lord doth come" (Matt. 24:37-42).

As to Noah, the faith which led him to build the ark and to enter it with his family made him patient and obedient to the will of God during the long months of his imprisonment. He waited one hundred and fifty days for the waters to decrease. Then the ark rested on the mountains of Ararat two and a half months; later the tops of the mountains appeared. Forty days later Noah sends forth from the ark a raven and a dove as messengers to bring him tidings of the reappearing land. The raven does not return. When the dove is sent forth a second time, seven days later, it returns bearing a fresh olive leaf. This leaf signified that the renewed earth was ready to receive Noah. Therefore the "olive branch" has been universally accepted as the symbol of peace. Seven days later the dove is sent forth and its failure to return indicates that food and shelter were found outside the ark.

In spite of these favorable signs, it was not until a month later, on New Year's day, that Noah removed the covering from the ark and saw that the ground was dried. He waited, however, eight weeks longer, until God gave the command to go forth out of the ark.

As part of this command, the words were repeated which had been spoken to Adam: "Be fruitful and multiply upon the earth," thus emphasizing the fact that a new race of men was to begin.

The first act of Noah was to erect an altar and to sacrifice burnt-offerings to the Lord, thus expressing gratitude for his salvation, and by this act of worship dedicating himself and his family to the service of

God. On His part, God accepts the offering and the worshipers and enters into a covenant with Noah. The nature of the covenant was that of a promise. It was made in free grace alone, before Noah had done anything to merit the blessing of God, except by his trust and obedience. The blessings were to extend even to the lower animals, and to include "every living creature" of the earth. It was in its essence a promise that there should not "any more be a flood to destroy the earth." It recognized the sacredness of human life. Murder should be regarded as a capital crime, and the necessity of human government be recognized: "Whoso sheddeth man's blood, by man shall his blood be shed." While flesh could be eaten, blood, the symbol of life, should be regarded as sacred to God. Above all, there was the assurance of the uniformity of law. Never again would there be such an interruption with the course of nature. Neither man nor his works would ever again be swept away by a flood. "While the earth remaineth, seed time and harvest, and cold, and heat, summer and winter, and day and night shall not cease" (Ch. 8:22).

The sign of the covenant was to be the rainbow. "I do set my bow in the cloud and it shall be for a token of a covenant between me and the earth." Noah had been familiar with this beautiful and striking object; but henceforth it would have for him a new significance. As is seemed to unite earth and heaven it might symbolize the loving relation between man and God. As it arched above the whole horizon it would show the all embracing scope of the covenant. Whenever Noah looked upon this lovely symbol he would be assured of the grace and care and faithfulness of God. It would be a token of promise and of hope.

The closing scene in the life of Noah is as surprising as it is distressing: "And Noah began to be a husbandman, and he planted a vineyard; and he drank of the wine and was drunken; and he was uncovered within his tent." Some have supposed that Noah was ignorant of the effects of wine and so became intoxicated without knowing his danger. More commonly, he is regarded as an example of the "detestable vice" of intemperance. If such be the case, his sin was grievous, and embodies a solemn warning. Here was a man who for centuries had "walked with God" lying naked on the floor of his tent in a drunken stupor. Here was a man who for years had been a preacher of righteousness overcome by the sin of intemperance, which curses his descendants to the present day. Here we see this new lord of creation unable to control the appetites of his own body.

How evident it is that neither rich experience nor the wisdom of old age make one immune from the assault of evil. How often one who has been a hero in scenes of dramatic and public importance falls helpless before the assaults of temper and selfishness in the privacy of his own home.

It is also true that neither memories, however tragic or sacred, nor responsibilities, however great, can keep one from sin. Noah had seen the destruction of a race, and had spent a year of solitude in fellowship with God, yet he now falls helpless before this common and vulgar vice.

Nothing but the grace of God, through faith in

Christ, can avail to give one victory over weakness and appetite and the power of evil habit. "Let him that thinketh he standeth take heed lest he fall." "Watch and pray lest ye enter into temptation."

The character of the three sons of Noah was revealed by the way in which they severally regarded the disgrace of their father. Ham looked upon the fallen, helpless, insensible figure without pity or sorrow. Possibly with the purpose of ridicule, he "told his two brethren without." On the other hand, Shem and Japheth, with reverent delicacy, "took a garment," and walking backward placed it as a covering on the sleeping form. The way in which men regard the sins of others is ever a touchstone of character. Those who regard drunkenness lightly as a mere subject of jest, those who enjoy looking on scenes of shame, whether in real life or in fiction, are the true sons of Ham, whether their faces are white or black. True charity seeks to hide the faults of others unless exposure is absolutely necessary. "Charity covers a multitude of sins" (I Peter 1:8).

When Noah awakes from his drunken sleep and learns what has been done, he pronounces on his sons a curse and a blessing. His words were more than the expression of a hope or a wish. They were in the nature of prophecy. The curse, however, rested not on Ham, but on his son Canaan. Whether he first had seen Noah and informed his father, or whether he was guilty of some more shameless and insulting act, is a mere matter of conjecture. It is predicted, and the prediction is three times repeated, that he would be "a servant of servants unto his brethren" and his descendants hold a degraded position among the nations.

To Japheth was predicted a great and glorious future, and it is true that from him were descended the great world powers of history and the strongest of modern nations. He was to derive from Shem a knowledge of God and of pure religion, which is possibly what is meant by the words, "He shall dwell in the tents of Shem." This preservation of the knowledge of the true God was the peculiar privilege of Shem, as possibly indicated by the phrase: "Blessed be the Lord God of Shem." The fullness of this blessing would be realized in the birth of that Son of Shem who would be the Redeemer of the world.

To these three sons of Noah the origin of all the peoples of the earth was traced: "Of them was the whole earth overspread" (Ch. 9:19). To the genealogies of these ancestors of the human race two chapters are largely devoted (Chs. 10, 11).

It should be remembered, however, that, strictly speaking, these are not genealogies. The record concerns not individuals but peoples. The names, usually, are not merely of men, but represent tribes or nations. Indeed, this section of Scripture has been described as a "table of the nations." It is of great value. In it are records of remote periods of which there is no other material so reliable for the study of history and geography. It comes down to a time when nations and kingdoms had been definitely organized and their boundaries fixed. It traces the origin of the human race to one family, and indicates something of the purpose and overruling providence of God. It is a commentary on the statement of Paul to the Athenians when he declares that God "who made the world and all things therein . . . hath made of one blood all nations of men for to dwell on all the face of the earth, and hath determined the times before appointed and the bounds of their habitation" (Acts 17:26).

This "table of the nations" is interrupted by only one brief narrative, which seems to show that men were again forgetful of God and rebelling against Him rather than seeking to "feel after him and find him" (Ch. 11:1-9). It is the story of *Babel*. The scene was "in a plain in the land of Shinar," that is, in Babylonia, or the lower portion of Mesopotamia. There it was determined to build a great city with a high tower. The materials were to be indestructible burnt brick, with bitumen or "slime" for mortar. The purpose was not to honor or worship God, but, first of all, to glorify man, to show his ability and self-sufficiency. "Let us make us a name" was the cry. The further and more practical purpose was to thwart the divine intention of dispersing the race over the world to bring fruitfulness and widespread civilization: "Let us make a name, lest we be scattered abroad upon the face of the whole earth." The enterprise was in accordance with the dangerous principle of centralization of power. There are certain advantages. When the individual sacrifices his rights to the state, when smaller nations are bound together to form one empire, the force of the united body may be brought to bear more efficiently in carrying out the will of the nation or of the ruler. However, such a concentration of power may result in tyranny, in oppression, and in a loss of liberty and of all the higher values of life. This is obviously true in case God is excluded from the plans and the purposes of the state or of the alliance of nations.

In the language of the story "the Lord came down to see the city and the tower," that is to say, God was deeply interested in the conduct and the purposes of men. The plan met with his displeasure. The introduction of diversity of speech counteracted the ambitious display of power, or the purpose of universal empire. "The Lord scattered them abroad from thence . . . and they left off to build the city; therefore is the name of it called Babel [or "confusion"]."

It has been noted in contrast that when a spiritual body was to be formed through faith in Christ, there was a divine "gift of tongues" by which His grace was proclaimed; and, further, that God does have a purpose of gathering men from every nation and language into the city which He has founded, a city of glory and of gold.

Evidently there was need of One who could bring men into a true union and into real fellowship with God. Thus it is notable that after the narrative of Babel the genealogy of Shem is resumed, for it is from his descendants that a man is selected who is to be the ancestor of Christ. The line of Shem reaches its climax and its glory in Abraham, the "Father of the Faithful." Through him the promised Seed, the Redeemer, was to be brought into the world. All those who put their trust in this Deliverer and accept His provision for salvation and His offer of new life will be like Noah, the father of Shem, who "prepared an ark to the saving of his house: by which he condemned the world and became heir of the righteousness which is by faith."

# IV

## *ABRAHAM*

GENESIS 11:27 TO 25:10

THE MOST IMPORTANT AND COLOSSAL CHARACTER TO appear on the stage of history, before the birth of our Lord, was Abraham of Ur of the Chaldees, son of Terah. To the men of his day, and judged by common standards of greatness, this would not be true. Abraham conquered no country, he ruled no nation, he composed no books, he enacted no laws, he created no monuments of art. His sphere of influence was solely that of religion. To him Christians, Mohammedans, and Jews look back in reverence as to the founder of their faiths. It is to Abraham that the world owes its belief in the one living and true God. His character and his career are summed up in two familiar phrases: Abraham was "the Friend of God," and "the Father of the Faithful."

With Abraham began a new chapter in the divine plan of redemption. A man was chosen to be the head of a family from which issued a favored race. Shut off from their idolatrous neighbors in a land of their own, this people developed their religious beliefs and customs; they maintained their primitive faith, and became the medium of divine revelation. They were narrow in their sympathies, often apostate, and

unfaithful; but through them was preserved for the
world the knowledge of God which finally reached its
climax in the person and work of Christ. This knowledge is the supreme concern of each individual and
of the human race, for, as the Saviour declared, "This
is life eternal, that they might know thee, the only
true God and Jesus Christ whom thou hast sent."

## THE CALL OF ABRAHAM [Ch. 12:1-9.]

The home of Abraham was in the fertile valley of the
Euphrates, in or, more probably, near the populous
city of Ur. The Chaldaeans had attained a high de-
gree of civilization, but were debased by the most
profligate rites of idol worship. In what way God
appeared to Abraham or how He voiced His command
we cannot conjecture, but the call was clear, "Get thee
out of thy country, and from thy kindred, and come
into the land, which I shall shew thee" (Acts 7:3).
It would seem that Terah, his father, shared with
Abraham the decision to obey the divine summons.
In fact, we read that "Terah took Abraham, his son,
and Lot the son of Haran his son's son, and Sarai his
daughter in law, his son Abraham's wife; and they
went forth with them from Ur of the Chaldees, to go
into the land of Canaan; and they came unto Haran,
and dwelt there" (Gen. 11:31).

The call which came to Abraham was essentially the
same as that which comes today to one who is urged
to become a follower of Christ or is asked to under-
take some new task in His service. For Abraham two
difficulties were involved: the first was the separation

from scenes and friends which were dear; the second
was the uncertainty as to the land whither he would
be led. So the summons to Christian life or service
usually involves separation and sacrifice, and the
greater difficulty of facing the mysterious future. Yet
the call always includes a promise. "Now the Lord
had said unto Abraham . . . I will make of thee a great
nation, and I will bless thee . . . and thou shalt be a
blessing . . . and in thee shall all families of the earth
be blessed" (Ch. 12:1, 2). On that promise Abraham
laid hold. He believed God. He faced the sacrifice
and the mystery. He knew that blessing would follow.
"By faith Abraham when he was called to go out into
a place which he should afterward receive for an inheritance obeyed; and he went out not knowing
whither he went" (Heb. 11:8). First, he accompanied
his father up the rich valley three hundred miles
northward to Haran. From thence, on the death of
Terah, he turned westward and plunged into the
desert. In his caravan were "Sarai his wife and Lot
his brother's son and all the substance they had gotten
in Haran; and they went forth to go into the land of
Canaan; and into the land of Canaan they came"
(Ch. 12:5).

Yet the life of faith does not consist of one act of
obedience or in a single journey to some distant scene.
It is an experience continually related to the unseen
and the eternal. Its symbol is a tent, its secret is an
altar. So it was with Abraham. "By faith he became
a sojourner in the land of promise, as in a land not
his own, dwelling in tents, with Isaac and Jacob, the
heirs with him of the same promise; for he looked for

the city which hath the foundations, whose builder and maker is God" (Heb. 11:9, 10. R.V.).

Thus Abraham, as a pilgrim, passed through the land, moving southward, and encamped first at Shechem, and then near to Bethel; "and there he builded an altar unto the Lord, and called upon the name of the Lord" (Ch. 12:8).

## THE IMPERFECTION OF FAITH [Ch. 12:10-20.]

The pilgrim life is not free from peril and from trial. Abraham is soon confronted with famine. He moves to Egypt where the overflowing Nile gives fertility to a land which need not depend on rain. The stranger from Canaan finds pasturage for his flocks and herds, but his own life is in danger. Knowing the immorality of the country, he fears that the men may kill him in order to seize his wife. Therefore he agrees with Sarai to say that she is his sister. This was a shameful half-truth. Sarai was the daughter of his father but not of his mother. The statement that she was his sister was made by Abraham to indicate that she was not his wife. A half-truth is often more deceptive and more injurious than a frank falsehood. It is always more contemptible. The issue was what might have been expected. The courtiers report to the king the unusual beauty of Sarai, and she is taken to the royal palace to be made a wife of Pharaoh. God mercifully intervenes. A strange malady attacks the royal household, and delays the marriage. The king is made to believe that it is a warning against a great if unintentional crime. His conduct reveals a sur-

prising dignity and restraint. He administers a severe
rebuke to Abraham, but he does not ask for a return
of the rich gifts he had made to assure his friendship
before he had learned of his deception. Then he dismisses Abraham and his wife that they may leave the
land. It may seem that Abraham escaped, suffering
no penalty, and that he had profited richly by his evil
course. Let no one so conclude. Probably Abraham
would have given all his great possessions if he could
erase from his memory the look of contempt he saw
on the face of Pharaoh, and the shame and chagrin
that he felt when, as a professed servant of God, he
had merited the scorn and reproof of a pagan king.

## The Separation from Lot [Gen. 13.]

When Abraham returned from Egypt to Canaan,
it almost might be said that he returned to God, at
least he could have enjoyed little divine fellowship in
the land to which he had fled in fear, and during those
disgraceful days when to insure his own safety he had
placed his wife in deadly peril. Now, chastened and
repentant, "he went on his journeys from the south
even to Bethel, unto the place where his tent had
been at the beginning . . . unto the place of the altar,
which he had made there at the first, and there Abraham called on the name of the Lord" (Ch. 13:3, 4).

However, here he is met by a new difficulty and
trial. This was in connection with his nephew Lot.
Both had become very rich, with great herds of sheep
and cattle. They found it difficult to secure sufficient
pasturage, the more so because available fields were

restricted, since "the Canaanite and the Perizzite dwelled then in the land." There was continual friction between the rival herdsmen of Abraham and Lot. Separation was inevitable. Therefore Abraham offered his nephew the choice of any region he might prefer, and agreed to accept for himself some remaining portion of the land. The least sense of propriety or modesty or gratitude should have inclined Lot to refuse so generous an offer. Abraham was the older man, to him the whole land had been promised, and from him Lot had received unmeasured favors. Yet in selfishness "Lot lifted up his eyes and beheld all the plain of Jordan, that it was well watered everywhere . . . even as the garden of the Lord. . . . Then Lot chose him all the plain of Jordan . . . and pitched his tent toward Sodom."

He entered on the enjoyment of the very best of the Land of Promise. There was only on defect, one great peril: "The men of Sodom were wicked and sinners before the Lord exceedingly." It was a fatal choice. Soon Lot is living in the city. He becomes prominent among the citizens. His daughters marry men of Sodom. He is carried captive by the king of Elam. As his wife seeks to flee from the doomed city she becomes a "pillar of salt." Lot ends his disgraceful career overwhelmed by crime in a foul mountainside cave.

Any choice is fatal which at the expense of moral risk regards merely selfish advantage and material gain.

The experience of Abraham forms an impressive contrast. He had not left the choice with Lot, not in reality. He had left the choice with the Lord. This

is to say, it was by faith that he allowed his nephew
to select whatever portion of the land he desired. He
knew that it all belonged to him, and that some day
God would fulfill His promise. No ingratitude or
selfishness could take from him the inheritance of
which God had spoken.

His reward was immediate. There came to him the
divine assurance: "Lift up thine eyes and look from
the place where thou art, northward and southward,
and eastward and westward: for all the land which
thou seest, to thee will I give it and to thy seed forever. And I will make thy seed as the dust of the
earth." Not to Lot and his descendants but to Abraham and his sons the Land of Promise was to belong.

In perfect peace of mind, confiding in the word of
God, Abraham could let Lot depart to the rich plains
of Jordan and to the city of Sodom; but Abraham
moved his tent to Hebron, "and built there an altar
unto the Lord." Far better it was to dwell in the
highlands, under the open skies, in fellowship with
God, and looking for the Celestial City, than to seek
a home among the palaces in the City of Destruction.

## ABRAHAM RESCUES LOT [Ch. 14.]

"The children of this world are in their generation
wiser than the children of light." Yet sometimes a
worldly-wise man, seeking material gain and indiffer-
ent to moral peril brings himself into difficulties from
which he can be delivered only by the help of some
heavenly-minded child of God. So it was with Lot.
He selfishly chose for himself the rich plain of the

Jordan; then he "pitched his tent toward Sodom"; then he becomes a resident in the foul city; then, when the rebellious king of Sodom and his four confederates are defeated in battle by Chedorlaomer, king of Elam, and his three allied kings, Lot, with the men of Sodom and all their goods, is carried away a helpless captive. Word is brought to Abraham, who is worshiping by his altar in Hebron. The aged patriarch immediately arms three hundred and eighteen of his servants. Supported by the forces of three neighboring chieftains, he pursues the retreating armies and overtakes them as they are burdened with booty. By a skillful and unexpected night attack he discomfits the bewildered warriors, pursues them far to the north, and rescues Lot and his companions.

No mention is made of any expression of gratitude on the part of Lot; but the king of Sodom met Abraham and offered him as a prize all the goods which had been taken from the city by the invading army. Abraham absolutely refuses a gift which comes from such a polluted source, but accepts some recompense to be shared among his confederate chieftains. As for himself, he declares: "I will not take from a thread to a shoelatchet . . . lest thou shouldest say, I have made Abram rich."

In contrast with the king of Sodom, Abraham, as he returns, is met by one of the most majestic and mysterious figures in all the Bible story. "Melchizdek king of Salem brought forth bread and wine; and he was priest of the most high God. And he blessed Abraham," and from Abraham he received tithes. As he was "King of Salem, which is King of peace,"

and "Melchizdek" which is "by interpretation King
of righteousness," he is taken as a significant type of
Christ, who is "our Righteousness" and the "King of
Peace" (Hebrews 7:1-25). No mention is made in
the narrative of his parents or pedigree, none of his
previous or subsequent career. He was not immortal;
but so far as this story goes, he had "neither beginning
of days nor end of life," and so illustrates the eternal
and changeless priesthood of our Lord. He received
tithes and therefore was recognized as superior to
Abraham, and so belonged to a higher order of priesthood than the sons of Aaron, who were descendants
of Abraham and were supreme among human media-
tors. He "blessed" the "Father of the Faithful" as
Christ alone can bless those who put their trust in
Him, for "He is able also to save them to the uttermost that come unto God by him, seeing he ever
liveth to make intercession for them." Melchizdek,
for the refreshment of Abraham, "brought forth
bread and wine"; so Christ has appointed for us in the
Holy Supper, like symbols of his High-priestly work.

## The Covenant with Abraham [Ch.15.]

Abraham was dispirited and despondent. Such is
the common supposition. There was reason for de-
pression. He had rescued Lot, but he had wounded
the pride of the great king of Elam, who, with an over-
whelming force, would certainly return, seeking revenge. Then, too, he had rebuffed the king of Sodom
and thus dimmed the prospect of obtaining possession
of the very best portion of the Land of Promise.

Then "the word of the Lord came unto Abram in a vision, saying, Fear not, Abram: I am thy shield, and thy exceeding great reward." If God was his "shield" he need not fear what man could do unto him. If God was his "reward" then he would find in the Lord enough to compensate him for any loneliness or loss.

Possibly the words should be rendered: "Thy reward shall be exceedingly great." Abraham answers plaintively: "Why give me a reward? No possession can be 'great' so long as I am childless and my servant Eliezer is to be 'mine heir.'" The answer came: "He shall not be your heir, but your own son shall be your heir." Then Abraham is pointed toward the stars which blazed innumerable in the clear Syrian sky, and he heard the promise, "So shall thy seed be."

"And he believed in the Lord and he counted it to him for righteousness." His faith was well pleasing to God, and he was counted righteous, not for any good works or for any rites or ceremonies, but only for his trust in God and for submission to God's will. Here is the statement and the gem of all the New Testament teaching concerning "justification by faith," and the issue of faith in a life of holiness. This is the basis for the argument of Paul in the fourth chapter of Romans, where he quotes this passage and concludes: "Therefore it was imputed to him for righteousness . . . but for us also to whom it shall be imputed if we believe on him that raised up Jesus our Lord from the dead" (Rom. 4:22, 24).

The faith of Abraham was not perfect; and it was not unnatural that he asks of the Lord some sign or pledge that the promise, now repeated, that the land is to be his will really be fulfilled.

The pledge given is twofold; first, a definite and detailed prediction relative to the seed to be born, and then a solemn rite to seal the promise of the land. The prediction came in the deep darkness of the night, appropriate to the character of the prophecy: The descendants of Abraham would dwell as strangers for four hundred years in the land of Egypt, and there suffer bitter bondage and affliction. When the iniquity of the inhabitants of Canaan was ripe for judgment, then Israel would be delivered from slavery and receive possession of the Land of Promise.

The solemn rite, by which the promise was ratified, consisted of placing the bodies of slain animals in two rows, between which the contracting parties passed, which was a familiar custom of the day in the solemn making of covenants. Abraham placed and passed between the bodies, and then, in the darkness, a blazing light, the visible symbol of Deity, passed between them. Thus it was that "in the same day the Lord made a covenant with Abram, saying, Unto thy seed have I given this land, from the river of Egypt unto the great river, the river Euphrates."

It was an act of divine condescension and grace for God to be willing to follow this human custom whereby fallible men gave assurance to their pledges. Infinitely greater is the grace whereby He seals to believers the promise of eternal life and a heavenly heritage by the work of Christ, who is the divine Mediator of a New Covenant by which we become heirs of an eternal inheritance.

### THE BIRTH OF ISHMAEL [Ch. 16.]

Much might be said in defense of Abraham, even when admitting his fault in taking as a wife the Egyptian slave girl Hagar. It must be remembered that it was a common custom to contract such a secondary marriage to insure the continuance of a family. Then, again, while Abraham had been promised a son, no assurance had been given that Sarai was to be the mother; and, further, the expedient of taking Hagar as a wife was proposed and urged by Sarai herself. There was, indeed, something of heroism on the part of Sarai in willingly giving to another what was most precious to her in life. However, it is true that both Abraham and Sarai lacked faith to wait in patience for God to fulfill His promise in His own time and way. They seemed to believe that God needed their wretched expedient in order that they might be the channels of blessing to the world. Yet the end does not justify improper means, and "whatsoever a man soweth, that shall he also reap."

To Abraham and Sarai the harvest of thorns and briars came with surprising speed. As soon as Hagar is aware that she is to give birth to a child she despises her mistress and treats her with insolence and scorn. This is more than the proud spirit of Sarai can endure. She reports to Abraham the conduct of her slave and in her irritation unreasonably blames him for the very situation she herself has created. "My wrong be upon thee: . . . the Lord judge between me and thee."

Abraham refuses to intervene between his wife and

her insolent servant. He bids Sarai to act as seems best, and she seems to feel that she is free to treat Hagar with such bitterness and cruelty that the slave girl flees into the wilderness toward her Egyptian home. As she pauses to rest by the well in an oasis she is found by "the angel of the Lord." This august title appears here for the first time in Scripture. Whether it denotes a visible appearance of the Son of God, or some angelic messenger who is commissioned to identify himself with Jehovah as His messenger, is not clear. Hagar is certain that she has received a divine command to return to her mistress, and she obeys. She is encouraged to this difficult course by such a new understanding of the presence and care of the Lord that she exclaims, "Thou God seest me," and the place is named "Beer-la-hai-roi" which possibly means "the well of the living and seeing God." To such a well many weary and discouraged wayfarers have come. Trusting in a God who is present, who knows, who sees, who loves, they turn back again to the places of duty, ready to face difficulty, reproach and distress.

Hagar was further encouraged by a specific divine prediction: she was to bear a son who would be the author of a great race which could "not be numbered for multitude." He would be named Ishmael ("God heareth") "because the Lord hath heard [her] affliction." "And he will be a wild man, his hand will be against every man, and every man's hand against him; and he shall dwell in the presence of all his brethren."

With remarkable literalness, this prediction of the three characteristics of the descendants of Ishmael has been fulfilled. The Bedouin Arabs have loved to dwell in the wilderness, delighting in freedom and scorning the comforts and restraints of settled communities. They have lived in continual enmity with one another and commonly have regarded others as natural foes or a welcome prey yet they have continued to "dwell in the presence of all their brethren," a distinct race with the same features and customs and character which have been inherited from their ancestor Ishmael.

When in process of time the promise of the angel to Hagar was fulfilled, Abraham began to reap the fuller harvest of his fatal sowing. Discord and distress entered into his household. There was begun a historic process of hatred and division among those who believe in the one living and true God, a division which has been marked by rivers of blood and has engendered cruelties which still darken the horizon of the world. Through his son Ishmael, Abram became the progenitor of the Mohammedan nations, and through Isaac the ancestor of Christians and Jews; and in the religion of Mohammed, Christianity still finds its most bitter and formidable rival. In taking Hagar as his wife Abraham divided not only his own family, but imperiled the peace and progress of nations yet unborn.

## The Covenant Renewed [Ch. 17.]

Thirteen years passed in silence. No new message came from God, and no new event was recorded in the life of Abraham. Then came a surprising revelation. The covenant was renewed with astonishing predictions and sealed with a sacramental rite. On the divine side the covenant consisted of promises so incredible as to prove a severe test of faith; on the human side it involved trust and obedience. Therefore, in renewing the covenant there came first a claim and a command: "I am the Almighty God; walk before me, and be thou perfect." As the omnipotent God, He would be able to fulfill whatever He might promise; and Abraham, as the other party to the covenant, must live in continual consciousness of the divine presence and in unfailing submission to the divine will.

When Abraham bows down in reverence he receives a new name. The meaning of the name is not quite clear. It seems, however, that he is to be known no longer as "Abram," "Exalted Father," but as Abraham, "Father of a Multitude." Furthermore, came the assurance of God's peculiar favor toward the descendants of Abraham, and the promise to them of the Land of Canaan as an "everlasting possession."

On the side of Abraham the covenant was to be sealed by the rite of circumcision to which his sons were to submit through all coming generations.

Then came the most astonishing promises. Sarah, who was now ninety years of age, was to bear a son. She was to become "a mother of nations." "Kings of people" were to be among her descendants. As a further sign of the covenant her name also was to be changed. It no longer was to be "Sarai," but "Sarah," a "princess," a mother of kings. In utter surprise and astonishment, "Abraham fell upon his face and laughed." He was overcome by what to human reason seemed absurd. Yet faith triumphed. He gave glory to God, "being fully assured that what he had promised he was able to perform" (Romans 4:21).

Mingled with his joy, there comes to Abraham a sense of sorrow as he thinks of his son Ishmael. Will the birth of the promised heir exclude Ishmael from all the inheritance Abraham had been intending for him? He cried out to God in his behalf: "O that Ishmael might live before thee!" The gracious reply is received, that he is to be richly blest and is to become the father of a great nation. However, the covenant is to be fulfilled through the son of Sarah. Her son is to be called Isaac, ("he laughs"), to recall the laughter of Abraham and to be a continual reminder that the birth of the true heir is to be so miraculous as to seem incredible to human reason. Through the son of the free woman and not of her bond servant all the nations of the world were to be blest. The covenant was sealed by the rite which had been prescribed. So those who accept Christ receive a corresponding seal in the sacrament of baptism, signifying that by faith they are "Abraham's seed, and heirs according to the promise."

## HOSPITALITY AND INTERCESSION [Ch. 18.]

The grace of hospitality never has been limited to any one race or time. Great stress is laid on it in the New Testament. Paul urged the Romans to be "given to hospitality" (Romans 12:13). John wrote two epistles bearing on this theme (I and II John). In

Hebrews (13:1) we have the exhortation, "Be not forgetful to entertain strangers: for thereby some have entertained angels unawares."

Of this last experience Abraham was a historic example. There is in his story a flavor of the Orient and of antiquity. As the aged patriarch is seated at the opening of his tent, in the sultry noonday, he is surprised by the appearance of three strangers. They are of impressive character, and one of them is closely identified with Jehovah. He is called "the Lord." Whether this again is to be regarded as an appearance of the Son of God, or whether some angelic creature was appointed to represent the Divine Being, it is difficult to assert. Nor is it clear to what extent Abraham was aware of the nature of his guests. The generous reception he gave them was peculiarly Oriental. He refers to his proffered entertainment in the humblest of terms. What he offers is merely "a little water" to wash their feet, and a "morsel of bread" to "comfort" their "hearts." What he really provides are cakes baked by Sarah from "three measures of fine meal" and the "tender and good" flesh of a fatted calf.

When they have been refreshed they make known the nature of their mission. They have come with a specific message concerning the heir that has been promised to Abraham. By divine power the promise was to be fulfilled, and Sarah, in spite of her advanced age, would bear a son. In feminine modesty Sarah was hidden in her tent; but her human curiosity led her to overhear all that was being said. At the absurdity of the prediction, "Sarah laughed within herself."

When taxed with her incredulity, she was asked, "Is anything too hard for the Lord?" and then she denied that she had laughed.

Sarah does not appear here in a very creditable light; but soon her doubt was dispelled, her faith in God returned, and she became a channel of blessing to the whole world: "Through faith also Sara herself received strength to conceive seed, and was delivered of a child when she was past age, because she judged him faithful who had promised. Therefore sprang there even of one, and him as good as dead, so many as the stars of the sky in multitude, and as the sand which is by the sea shore innumerable" (Heb. 11:11, 12).

In sudden and striking contrast with this promise of blessing is a divine prediction of the approaching doom of Sodom. It was natural that the purpose of God should be revealed to Abraham his "Friend" (James 2:23, John 15:15). However, two reasons are given for this disclosure. It had been promised that in Abraham "all the nations of the earth should be blessed." Some explanation was needed to prepare his mind for the disaster which was about to fall on great cities so near to his own abode.

In the second place, Abraham was to become the ancestor of a great people to whom a glorious destiny was promised on condition of their obedience to the Lord. They needed an object lesson of the destruction which would inevitably fall on those who failed "to do justice and judgment." Through all their history that people was blinded by the belief that the promised blessings of God were independent of moral fitness, and that being the children of Abraham was sufficient to assure the abiding favor of God. The doom of Sodom should have reminded them that "the wages of sin is death."

Abraham is assured, however, that God will never punish without a full and accurate knowledge of guilt. He first would "go down" and would "see whether" the report of the iniquity of Sodom was true. However, Abraham knew, and the Lord indicated, that the verdict was certain. The day of judgment had come. Therefore Abraham intercedes for Sodom. He does not plead for mercy, but for justice. He thinks of his relative Lot and of others who possibly may not have yielded to the abominable iniquity of Sodom. Would it be right for God to "destroy the righteous with the wicked"? There might be "fifty righteous within the city," and should not the Lord "spare the place for the fifty righteous"? Nor is the plea of Abraham made merely with the thought of Lot. He is jealous for the name of the Lord. He shrank from the thought of injustice being ascribed to God. "Shall not the Judge of all the earth do right?"

God graciously grants the request and promises to spare the city if fifty righteous be found in the place. Abraham is emboldened by the promise and asks that the whole city shall be spared if forty-five righteous persons can be found therein; then if forty, then thirty, then twenty, then ten. And the Lord said, "I will not destroy it for ten's sake." This was a notable example of humble, yet persevering and prevailing prayer. It can even be regarded as throwing a gleam of light on the intercession of our Lord. He pleads for us, not merely on the ground of mercy, but on the ground of justice. In view of His atoning work, God can be "just, and the justifier of him which believeth in Jesus." "Who is he that condemneth: It is Christ that died, yea rather, that is risen again, who is even at the right hand of God, who also maketh intercession for us." "He is able also to save them to the uttermost that come unto God by him, seeing he ever liveth to make intercession for them."

## The Fate of Lot [Ch. 19.]

Had ten righteous persons been found in Sodom the city would have been spared. These could not be discovered and the dread judgment fell. Whatever natural causes may have been employed, the doom of Sodom was regarded as a divine visitation. No justification need be sought. There was nothing hasty or inconsiderate in the act. God had "come down" to see. The foul guilt of the place was beyond all question. This corruption was like a cancer certain to be fatal, and the end of the city was only hastened by its sudden doom. Then, too, its destruction was a warning needed by the human race. No other catastrophe in history came to be used so frequently as a merciful if appalling warning that "the wages of sin is death."

The interest of the story centers, however, not in the multitudes of the perishing cities but in the fate of Lot the nephew of Abraham. The scene has shifted with sudden contrast. There was Abraham seated at noonday under the shade of his oak tree, enjoying divine fellowship. Here is Lot, as the hideous night deepens, besieged in his city home by an infuriated mob of demons, his fellow citizens of Sodom. For years Abraham has walked with God, in separation from the world, living as a pilgrim and a stranger, even in the Land of Promise. Lot has been willing to imperil his soul in seeking earthly advancement and material gain. His downward course has been rapid. First, there was his selfish choice of the better portion of the land; then he "pitched his tent toward Sodom," knowing the perilous corruption of the city. Now we find him seated in the gate of the city, a place of prominence, and advantage and probable influence. Two strangers appear. To protect them from possible violence, and to show them hospitality, he persuades them to enter his home, and learns that he, too, is entertaining "angels unawares." When an impassioned mob assaults the house, he endeavors to insure the safety of his guests by a foul compromise. He even ventures out alone to meet the assailants. He is saved from death by the two angels, who draw him into the house and smite the mob with blindness. He is told of the immediate doom of the city and urged to warn his relatives to flee. His words seem to be those of a madman. No one believes him. By main force, the angels lead out Lot and his wife and his two daughters from the scene of impending doom. They are bidden to make haste and not to look backward. Lot's wife, not in mere curiosity, but with a longing for all the comforts and luxury she has enjoyed "looks back" and is (transferred into) a "pillar of salt." Lot wishes for something also of what has been his in the guilty city. He pleads for the privilege of tarrying in the "little city of Zoar." This, however, is not a place of safety. His flight ends in a mountain cave, where he lives with his daughters. There, stupefied with wine, he is implicated in a monstrous crime, and becomes the progenitor of the Moabites and Ammonites, who were to prove the continual enemies of the descendants of Abraham.

The character of Lot is composed of conflicting factors. Yet in it there is little to admire. In the New Testament he is called a "righteous" man. This is a comparative term. He did not yield to the abominable corruption of the men among whom he lived; yet his whole life seemed controlled by the motive of selfishness. Hoping for material gain, he was willing to live in surroundings of moral corruption, where he was "vexed with the filthy conversation of the wicked" (II Peter 2:8). Better far to sojourn, as did Abraham, far from the scenes of iniquity, there to dwell in peace and look for "the city which hath foundations whose builder and maker is God."

## ABRAHAM AND ABIMELECH [Ch. 20.]

It is said rightly that one reason for accepting the Bible stories as true is found in the fact that the authors never seek to hide the grievous faults and failures of their heroes. On the other hand, a great moral weakness in even such a majestic character as Abraham is a warning to all the children of God to walk humbly and to heed the words of the apostle: "Let him that thinketh he standeth take heed lest he fall."

After his long sojourn in Hebron, Abraham had moved toward the south, and had encountered the Philistines, then a tribe far less numerous and more peaceable than their descendants, who became the hereditary foes of Israel. Fearing that he would be killed in order that Sarah might be seized, he resorted to the same cowardly subterfuge that he had used twenty years before with Pharaoh, in Egypt: "He said of Sarah his wife, She is my sister." This half-truth might insure his safety, but it placed Sarah in imminent peril. "And Abimelech king of Gerar sent and took Sarah."

That at her age she could have been attractive to the king seems incredible, yet it must be remembered that her physical vigor had been so preserved or restored that within a year she bore a child, and further that Abimelech may have wished merely to form an alliance with such a rich and powerful chieftain as Abraham seemed to be.

In any event, God smote Abimelech and his people with a plague, and then, in a dream, explained this punishment and warned Abimelech of his peril. The king immediately summons Abraham and administers a dignified but severe rebuke to him. In attempting to excuse himself, Abraham reveals the real explanation of his sin. He had made a compact with Sarah, early in their lives, that whenever it seemed necessary they would unite in the falsehood, which was more dangerous because half true. So the moral fall of many children of God can be traced to some wrong principle or promise which, long concealed, lingers in the heart and on some occasion brings forth its bitter and shameful fruit.

Abimelech not only restores to Abraham his wife but presents to him a princely gift, including a thousand pieces of silver. In turning to Sarah with a courteous and deserved reproof, he refers to this silver as a means to make all parties concerned blind to his fault: "It is to thee [rather than "he is to thee"] a covering of the eyes unto all that are with thee, and with all other."

In the vision Abraham had been called a "prophet," that is, a man who has special communion with God. So, as the story closes, Abraham prays for the healing of Abimelech and his house.

Abraham seems to have escaped with no punishment and rather to have been enriched by his fault. The divine justice will be questioned only by one who unlike Abraham has never known the unspeakable humiliation of appearing to live by a lower moral standard than the Philistines while claiming to be a child of God. There is no anguish of soul more distressing than that of a Christian who realizes that his conduct has brought contempt on his profession and dishonor on his Lord.

## THE SON OF THE BONDWOMAN [Ch. 21:1-21.]

In process of time the surprising promise was fulfilled. To the aged parents Abraham and Sarah a son was born. He received the divinely appointed name "Isaac." The term indicates "laughter." When Abraham received the promise he had laughed, possibly in mingled joy and surprise. When the same message came to Sarah she had laughed with more obvious incredulity; when the promise was fulfilled she cried in ecstasy, "God hath made me to laugh, so that all that hear will laugh with me." Possibly there was a deeper meaning in that name. The child was to bring joy to the parents. His character was to be cheerful and happy. Then, too, it was realized by the father that from this son the One was to be born who would be the Saviour, the Joy of the whole earth. Is not this the meaning of the Master when he says: "Your father Abraham rejoiced to see my day, and he saw it and was glad"? (John 8:56).

Yet the birth of Isaac was the occasion, not only of rejoicing, but of bitterness, of envy, and of dire distress. The prospects and expectations of Ishmael are suddenly shattered. He had grown to youthful vigor, confident that he was to inherit the great wealth and power of his father. Now the true heir appears. Ishmael is moved to mad hatred. Proud and impetuous, he does not conceal his chagrin. On the occasion of a great feast given in honor of Isaac he is guilty of insolence, of mockery and insult. Sarah is infuriated at this gross disrespect shown to her as well as to Isaac. She demands that Abraham shall immediately expel Hagar and her son. She cried out with words which have become historic: "Cast out this bondwoman and her son: for the son of the bondwoman shall not be heir with my son, even with Isaac."

Abraham had come to love Ishmael. There was much that was admirable in this audacious, bold adventurous youth. It required a divine message to make

Abraham accede to the demand of Sarah. He was assured that only in Isaac could the promises be fulfilled, and he was to be recompensed in the fact that "of the son of the bondwoman" God would make a great nation.

The request of Sarah was spiteful. The method of carrying out her purpose was cruel. Yet the separation involved was absolutely necessary. Hagar and Ishmael are thrust out into the wilderness, helpless and in deadly peril. Even though divinely guided and rescued, they had suffered injustice and needless harshness and distress.

However, they could have remained no longer in the family of Abraham. Hatred and dissension would have increased; tragedy might have ensued. It was impossible that Isaac and Ishmael should both be the real heirs of Abraham. As God declared: "In Isaac shall thy seed be called."

This distressing scene throws into bold relief the fact that the true child of promise had been born. It was to the son of Sarah and not to the son of Hagar that the inheritance was to come. He and only he would be the source of blessing to the whole world.

This scene also furnishes Paul with the features of his famous allegory (Galatians 4:21-31). Ishmael was a child of the flesh, whose birth was due to a poor human expedient. Isaac was a child of faith, born in accordance with a divine promise and through dependence on God. So the true heirs of Abraham are not those who are such "after the flesh" but those who through faith in Christ are "heirs according to promise." There cannot be two ways of salvation, works and faith, law and grace. Both Ishmael and Isaac could not have been the true heirs of Abraham. To seek to be saved by our own deeds and in obedience to law is to make ourselves children of the bondwoman Hagar. To accept salvation as a gift of grace, through faith in Christ, is to become children of the free woman, and true heirs of Abraham.

Ritual and creed and morality are not the grounds of our acceptance with God. They may express our faith; but it is by faith we are saved. Let us not confuse law and grace. "In Isaac shall thy seed be called." "Cast out the bondwoman and her son: for the son of the bondwoman shall not be heir with the son of the freewoman." "Now we, brethren, as Isaac was, are the children of promise" (Galatians 4:28).

## Beersheba [Ch. 21:22-34.]

The sojourn of Abraham at Beersheba forms a long and lovely interlude between the distressing dismissal of Ishmael and the tragic offering of Isaac. Probably here at Beersheba Isaac had been born. Here he spent his youth and early manhood. For Abraham it was a time of prosperity and peace. Of these quiet years only one incident is related. This was the ratifying of a treaty between Abraham and Abimelech. This was not merely a personal and private agreement. It was rather a formal alliance between two tribal chieftains. Abraham had moved southward from Hebron to the very border of the Philistine territory. The king, Abimelech, recognizes the increasing power of this neighboring sojourner, to whom previously he had shown great kindness. He so declares to Abraham, "God is with thee in all that thou doest." Therefore he desires to make a covenant of peace to be binding on both parties and on their descendants.

Abraham takes occasion to tell the king of a wrong that had been done him. The servants of Abimelech had violently dispossessed Abraham of a well which he had dug and which was of great value. The king denied all knowledge of the wrong, which he recognized; and in formulating the treaty a clause was inserted to the effect that the well was the property of Abraham.

The covenant was solemnly sealed by the exchange of gifts and the offering of sacrifices. A special feature of the ceremony was the presentation by Abraham to Abimelech of "seven ewe lambs" as a token and acknowledgment that the well belonged to Abraham. Therefore the place was called "Beersheba," meaning either the "well of the oath," or the "well of the seven," as the oath was ratified by seven gifts.

There Abraham planted a tree (a "grove") as a memorial of the covenant. There too he established a shrine, "and called there on the name of the Lord, the everlasting God."

It is not unnatural that many readers have found in this description a possible parable picturing the Christian believer dwelling in peace, with confidence in the New Covenant, drawing refreshment from the well of the inspired word, and enjoying fellowship with God.

### THE PERFECTION OF FAITH [Ch. 22.]

The story of the supreme trial of Abraham's faith and of its matchless triumph is recorded by the New Testament writer in words as familiar as they are revealing: "By faith Abraham, when he was tried, offered up Isaac; and he that had received the promises offered up his only begotten son, of whom was said, That in Isaac shall thy seed be called; accounting that God was able to raise him up, even from the dead; from whence also he received him in a figure" (Heb. 11:17-19).

The trial was incomparably severe, not only that it required the sacrifice of an innocent life. Such an act must have been abhorrent, and yet Abraham could not have believed it was wrong. God may allow us to be severely tested, but He never commands us to do what we know to be sinful. "God cannot be tempted of evil, neither tempteth he any man" (James 1:13). It is possible that human sacrifice was so well known to Abraham that it was less abhorrent to him than it is to us. When the command came, he believed that, however dreadful, it was the will of God.

Nor did the severity of the trial consist chiefly in the fact that the life to be taken was that of an only son. This was appalling. It is emphasized by the words of the divine message: "Take now thy son, thine only son Isaac, whom thou lovest . . . and offer him for a burnt offering." Yet the esence of the trial lay in the fact that God seemed to contradict God. The promise was, "In Isaac shall all the nations of the world be blest"; then the command came, "Take thy son . . . and offer him for a burnt offering." How could the command be reconciled with the promise? Abraham naturally might have waited for some further light to solve the problem; but faith triumphed. He who believed God's promise obeyed God's command. He did so promptly and without delay. "Abraham rose up early in the morning and took Isaac his son and clave the wood for the burnt offering and rose up and went unto the place of which God had told him." For three days he has endured the torture of the journey. Without faltering, he climbs with Isaac the hill of sacrifice; he builds the simple altar; he binds his obedient son, and lifts his knife to plunge it into the victim's breast. Then came the arresting cry: "Lay not thine hand upon the lad, neither do thou anything unto him."

The sacrifice was complete, but the life was spared. God desired not the son of Abraham, but Abraham's submission. Why? What was the divine purpose? It was for the good of Abraham. Not, as many suppose, did God try Abraham to see whether Abraham would stand the test. God, in advance, knew what the issue would be. The Omniscient does not need to resort to experiments in order to increase His knowledge. If God allows us to be tempted it is not for His benefit, but for ours. To Abraham himself was revealed his inmost spirit; he discovered by actual experience that he held nothing more dear than the will of God; and to all, who by faith are the children of Abraham, there comes this thrilling example of triumphant trust, and the assurance that where there

is complete surrender to God, there will be deliverance
and renewed blessing.

God never intended that Isaac should die. Abraham sees "a ram caught in a thicket by his horns."
This he offered "for a burnt offering instead of his
son." Henceforth the place was called "Jehovah-Jireh,"
"The Lord will provide." Only when one has climbed
the mount of sacrifice, only when the complete surrender has been made, does one find the provision
God has made, and the gracious issue which God has
in store.

Six times there had come a divine promise to Abraham; now this seventh time, in the hour of supreme
victory, the promise is made complete. Abraham is
assured that his seed is to be numberless, that it is to
be victorious over all enemies, and that in this seed
all nations of the earth are to be blessed (Ch. 22:
16-18).

How did Abraham triumph? What was the secret
of his incomparable victory? It was "by faith." Yet
how did faith operate? This was the problem: God
had promised to bless the world through Isaac and
now God demands the life of Isaac. There was but
one solution. God would raise Isaac from the dead
"from whence also [Abraham] received him in a figure." He had surrendered his son to God; when Isaac
was returned to Abraham it was like a resurrection.
Thus by faith we surrender to God what we hold
most dear, confident that what God takes from us He
surely will restore.

The whole incident of the offering of Isaac is properly regarded as a figure, a parable. We know of a

Father who so loved the world that He gave His only begotten Son, that we might have eternal life. The death and resurrection of our Lord are divine realities, and should strengthen our faith in the unfailing love and gracious providence of God. In time or in eternity He will show us the blessed issue of our faith. He will recompense our every sacrifice. He will supply our every need. "He that spared not his own Son but delivered him up for us all, how shall he not with him also freely give us all things?" (Rom. 8:32).

## Machpelah [Ch. 23.]

Abraham had "intimations of immortality," even of resurrection. This was not the clear vision granted to believers to whom Christ has "brought life and immortality to light in the Gospel." However, he believed that "God was able to raise up even from the dead." "He looked for a city that hath foundations whose builder and maker is God." He believed that God "is not a God of the dead but of the living" and that from his "Friend" death could take nothing which would not be restored.

These truths must have comforted the aged patriarch when he looked for the last time on the face of Sarah as she lay asleep in death. Yet his grief was real and bitter. For the only time in his history it is recorded that he "wept." These were not tears of rebellion or regret or weakness. For more than seventy years these two had been partners in trials and hardships, in unique promises and hopes and blessings. Now the separation has come, no less painful for being so long delayed. His sorrow was the truest expression of his love.

The truths which comforted Abraham may also explain his deep concern to find a fitting burial place for the precious body of the dead. He had selected a field near to his home in Hebron. In it, surrounded by trees, was a cave well fitted to provide a natural sepulcher. The property belonged to Ephron, "who dwelt among the children of Heth." The story of the ceremonious purchase of this field vividly pictures the princely dignity of Abraham and reveals the very secrets of his heart. To us who are not familiar with Oriental customs and courtesies there is in the picture even a touch of humor. When Abraham mentions to the "sons of Heth" his desire to secure a burying place, they at once reply that he can make a choice among all the sepulchers they own; they will give it to him freely. He expresses a desire for a particular field, which he wishes to secure by purchase from its owner Ephron. Then Ephron offers to transfer it to Abraham as a gift. Abraham insists that he must "give money for the field." Ephron then states what he regards as the value of the field, but adds, "What is that betwixt me and thee?" "A mere four hundred shekels of silver is only a trifle between two such wealthy men." So in the presence of "the children of Heth" the bargain is signed and sealed "and the field and the cave therein were made sure unto Abraham for a possession of a burying place."

This purchase of the "cave of Machpelah" revealed not only the courtesy of Abraham and his deep affection, but also his far-seeing faith. He knew that he was not in person to possess the Land of Promise. After residing there for sixty or more years he did not own a portion large enough to provide a grave. In effecting the purchase of Machpelah he confessed to the "sons of Heth," "I am a stranger and a sojourner with you." He knew also that his descendants were to endure four hundred years of bitter bondage in a foreign country (Gen. 15:13). Yet the eye of faith looked into the distant future. He saw the day when the promises would be fulfilled, and when his "seed" would possess the land. Of that possession the field of Machpelah was the pledge. This was his own, and it became "the earnest" of his "inheritance." Even beyond the fulfillment of that dream he saw a "better country that is an heavenly," in which he was to be at home. Of such believers "God is not ashamed to be called their God: for he hath prepared for them a city."

Thus faith, even at the tomb of buried hopes, looks in confidence to the fulfillment of God's promises, and sees, through the darkness of bereavement, a vision of the walls of jasper and the gates of pearl, the glory of the Celestial City "whose builder and maker is God."

## The Death of Abraham [Ch. 25:1-10.]

Abraham survived the death of Sarah his wife by some forty years. These were years of a quiet, uneventful pastoral life, years of peace with his neighbors and continued prosperity. His interest and affection centered in Isaac his son, on whom he bestowed all his great wealth. The beautiful idyl of the marriage of Isaac and Rebekah belongs rather to the story of the son than of the aged father (Gen. 24). However, the part played by Abraham is important and completely in accord with his character as the great hero of faith. When he sent his servant to secure a bride for his son, Abraham insisted on two significant conditions: first, the maiden must not come from the idolatrous people among whom Abraham was dwelling as a sojourner; secondly, Isaac must not leave the Land of Promise lest he be tempted to remain among his kindred in the home of the prospective bride. Abraham regarded the land of Canaan as his real inheritance and the certain possession of his heirs. He had the deep satisfaction of welcoming Rebekah from her distant home as a beloved daughter.

It seems that in the course of years Abraham himself "took a wife and her name was Keturah." Her six sons became the progenitors of Arab tribes whose country lay between the Persian Gulf and the Red Sea.

At last the long pilgrimage came to its end. For one hundred years the aged patriarch had "sojourned in the Land of Promise as in a strange country"; now the time had come when he was to see more clearly that City of God for which he had been looking. After "an hundred three score and fifteen years" he "died in a good old age, an old man and full of years, and was gathered to his people." His two sons, Isaac and Ishmael, followed him in reverence and affection as his body was laid to rest in the cave of Machpelah. In like reverence countless thousands have turned in memory toward that place of burial. Abraham is regarded rightly as a figure of unsurpassed dignity and grandeur. He is so regarded, not for his wealth or his princely character, but as one who believed the promises of God and acted wholly on that belief. His epitaph is plainly engraved: "The Father of the Faithful, The Friend of God."

# V

## ISAAC

THE FIGURE OF EVEN A GREAT MAN MAY BE DWARFED by comparison with that of a distinguished father or of a famous son. Thus the character of Isaac is overshadowed by the majesty of Abraham and the dramatic interest of Jacob. There was a third factor which diminished the importance of Isaac; he was the husband of a clever and masterful wife. No matter how exciting the scene in which he may appear, he always was assigned to a minor part. At least, by contrast with these other actors, his rôle in life was prosaic, uneventful, obscure. However, there was much that was beautiful, even admirable, about Isaac. He was pure, generous, affectionate, and was guided by unquestioning faith in God. And as he stepped on the stage in the first dramatic act of his life he exhibited a heroism almost unsurpassed (Ch. 22).

His father Abraham had determined that the life of his beloved son must be offered as a sacrifice to God. Together they journeyed to the appointed place, together they climbed the mountain, when suddenly the purpose of his father was revealed to Isaac. He was assured that his death was to be according to the divine will. In the strength of his vigorous young manhood he easily could have resisted and overcome Abraham. Yet there was no rebellion, no remonstrance. In complete submission he allowed himself to be bound, and to be laid on the wood which he had carried to the place of sacrifice. Without a murmur, he steeled his heart to receive the fatal blow of the uplifted knife. Then came the voice, "Lay not thine hand upon the lad," and then appeared the "ram caught in a thicket," the offering God had prepared. However, Isaac in reality had laid down his life in obedience to his father and in submission to God. He had shown himself worthy to be regarded as a type of that Son who carried His cross up Mount Calvary, and, yielding to the will of His Father, gave His life "a ransom for many." Indeed, Isaac is the ideal *symbol* of "*sonship*." Into that high estate those who put their trust in Christ now enter. The Redeemer was "sent forth . . . that we might receive the adoption of sons." We are no more servants but sons and heirs of God through Christ. As all the promises made to Abraham, and all his wealth, were bestowed on Isaac, so all the promises of God and all the riches of grace are ours if we "are Christ's, for Christ is God's." Let us, then, not live as slaves but as sons, in close fellowship with our Father and as heirs of his glory (Gal. 4:4-7).

As in the first scene of his life, Isaac manifested sublime heroism, so in his next appearance he is one of the heroes whose names are associated with a romance of such beauty that it holds a foremost place in the literature of the world (Ch. 24). This "betrothal of Isaac and Rebekah" is commonly regarded as the most charming idyl of the East. Here, however, as might be expected, Isaac is merely a passive figure in the scene. Everything is being managed for him. This was quite natural. Isaac was always being managed. For forty years he was managed by his father, then he was married, and for the rest of his life he was managed by his wife. He showed his obedience to his father in refraining, for so many years, from marrying any princess in Canaan, and he revealed his trust in God by accepting with such abiding affection the bride whom providence at length provided.

This betrothal was of supreme importance, for an heir of Isaac was to become the Saviour of the world. The chief interest and value of the story as recorded in Genesis consists in the lessons it contains in the matter of *divine guidance*. Among these we may note the following:

(1) If one is to learn the will of God he must believe that the guidance of God is not a matter of imagination or mysticism or sentiment, but an actual experience in daily life. So Abraham believed. When his servant was being sent on his difficult mission to the distant home of Abraham's relatives to secure a bride for Isaac, this servant naturally suggested that the woman of his selection might not be willing to accompany him to a strange land to marry a man she never had seen. Abraham replied: "The Lord God of heaven . . . he shall send his angel before thee, and thou shalt take a wife unto my son from thence." So at the end of his long journey the servant could say, "I being in the way the Lord led me." So, too, when

the father and brother of Rebekah had heard the story of the servant, they answered, "The thing proceedeth from the Lord; we cannot speak unto thee bad or good." So today we surely must believe that "as many as are led by the Spirit of God, they are the sons of God" (Rom. 8:14). Our perplexed hearts need to be cheered by the music of the Psalm, "The Lord is my shepherd. . . . He leadeth me" (Ps. 23).

(2) We are guided by the Word of God. Abraham gave specific directions to his servant. No bride could be selected from the daughters of Canaanites; one must be chosen from the country and kindred of Abraham. This narrowed the choice down to a very small area. It excluded large numbers of apparently eligible young women with whom Isaac may have been acquainted, and it confined the choice to a single family in a small city or town. So while the Bible does not answer every specific question which confronts us, it does narrow the circle of the problems we meet in daily life by excluding many choices which are shown to be contrary to the will of God.

(3) Conscience also is an instrument by which God makes known His will to us. This faculty is not infallible; it needs to be enlightened by the word of God; it cannot tell us what is right and what is wrong. Yet, in another sense it is infallible; it always tells us whether we intend to do what we believe to be right or what we believe to be wrong. In the sphere of moral intention it speaks with absolute authority. So when the servant had been told the will and purpose of Abraham, he bound himself by a solemn oath to follow his master's command. He was not free to

make any contrary choice. Thus, when conscience has been enlightened by the word of God, the problems of life must be faced with an absolute determination to obey its voice.

(4) We must pray for guidance if we are to learn the will of God. That is a picture as beautiful as it is instructive, the picture of the aged servant who has ended his long journey to Haran, the city of Abraham and Nahor, and now at eventide bows in prayer beside the well at the city gates. Probably the name of the servant was Eliezer (Ch. 15:2). The name means "God is a helper." Surely he is presented to us as one who, when facing a supreme decision in life, turns to God in earnest petition. He wishes to make the right choice for the sake of his master Abraham and of Abraham's son Isaac. While he was praying, even "before he had done speaking," his prayer was answered in the lovely person of Rebekah, who, quite unconscious of the fateful hour, "came out . . . with her pitcher on her shoulder," and, as the historian adds, "the damsel was very fair to look upon." Prayer does involve mysteries; but our Master gives us His divine encouragement, "Your Father knoweth what things ye have need of before ye ask him. . . . Ask, and it shall be given you" (Matt. 6:8; 7:7).

(5) However, we must exercise reason and common sense. It is almost amusing to note the shrewdness of that wise old servant Eliezer. He has asked God to confirm by a sign any choice he may make. He selects no arbitrary sign. He does not depend on chance. The bride he selects for Isaac must be beautiful, "very fair to look upon." She must be strong

and vigorous; Rebekah shows that she is able to water ten thirsty camels. Above all she must be kind, generous, obliging, even courteous to strangers; so when Eliezer makes his request, "Let me I pray thee drink a little water of thy pitcher," she replies in the very words included in his prayer as a sign, "Drink, my lord . . . and I will draw water for thy camels also." Thus, when he learns that Rebekah is of the kindred of Abraham, it is not surprising that Eliezer lifts his voice in thanksgiving: "Blessed be the Lord God of my master."

(6) Prompt obedience is necessary. We must take the next step as that step is revealed. The task of Eliezer was not ended. He must persuade the family as well as Rebekah that she is the bride divinely chosen for Isaac. He acts with surprising promptness. Indeed, the whole story is one of rapid motion. We read, "The servant ran to meet her"; "she ran again to the well"; "the damsel ran and told them of her mother's house"; and "Laban ran out unto the man, unto the well." So Eliezer, when he reached the house, refused to eat until he had told his errand. When the desired decision has been made, he declines, on the following morning, to tarry even "a few days." He must leave at once with the promised bride. He will not delay a single day.

(7) Submission to the will of God is the supreme condition of divine guidance. How does Rebekah make the most important decision in her life? Not merely in a spirit of adventure, to enjoy the romance of going to wed a stranger in a distant land; not only to please her parents; not because of the great wealth

of Isaac, which was evidenced by the ten camel loads of gifts, a factor which would have weight with a man like Laban. It was because, when she had heard the whole story from Eliezer, and had learned how her own words and acts had answered his prayer to God, she believed her decision was in accordance with the divine will and purpose. It was this which led her to say: "I will go."

A decision reached under the guidance of God is certain to result in blessing. At the end of the journey to Canaan, Isaac is found waiting for his lovely bride, waiting in prayerful meditation, at eventide, waiting in calm dependence on the goodness of God. His faith found its rich reward. Rebekah proved to be a woman peculiarly fitted to attract Isaac and to supplement his character. Her eager, ardent, active, enterprising spirit supplied the stimulus and inspiration needed by his quiet, contemplative, affectionate, passive temper. The disposition of each was exactly calculated to supplement that which the other lacked. For years their lives were blest by mutual devotion and love.

When Abraham died, "in a good old age, an old man, and full of years," he bequeathed his great wealth to his son, and Isaac continued to prosper and to enjoy the blessing of God (Ch. 25:8-11).

There was, however, one deep shadow on the happiness of Isaac and Rebekah. Twenty years had passed and no heir had been born to him through whose promised Seed all nations were to be blest. Then "Isaac intreated the Lord for his wife," and to these believing parents were born two sons, Jacob and Esau,

Waiting on God

whose turbulent lives were to have a wide influence on the history of the world.

After another lapse of years occurred an incident which revealed certain defects in the character of Isaac. His life had been free from recorded blemish, but he now falls before the very temptation to which his father Abraham had yielded on two separate occasions. Driven southward by famine, Isaac apparently planned to seek refuge in Egypt, but in obedience to God he remained in the Land of Promise, and sojourned in Gerar, to the southwest of Beer-sheba. God rewarded his obedience by renewing to him the promises of blessing made to his father Abraham. Here, however, while the promises of God were clearly in mind, Isaac is found guilty of cowardice and deceit. "The men of the place asked him of his wife; and he said, She is my sister: for he feared to say, She is my wife; lest said he, the men of the place should kill me for Rebekah; because she was fair to look upon" (Ch. 26:7).

The deception was long concealed, but when discovered by Abimelech, the king, Isaac was severely rebuked. He had no word to say in his defense, and must have experienced the bitter chagrin and humiliation which are felt by a professed servant of God when convicted of duplicity by an unprincipled Philistine.

This episode seems not to have affected the relationship existing between Abimelech and Isaac. The sojourner at Gerar was allowed to reap rich harvests of grain and to increase his vast possessions of flocks and herds. This marvelous prosperity on the part of this stranger aroused the jealousy of his neighbors, who showed their hostility by stopping with earth the very wells which, in other years, Abraham had dug. Abimelech sees the peril of violence and conflict and urges Isaac to withdraw to a greater distance from the city of Gerar. Isaac makes no remonstrance but retires to the valley of Gerar. There his servants dug a well, but the herdmen of Gerar claimed the water as their own. Isaac named the well "Esek" ("strife") and peacefully withdrew farther eastward. A second well, dug by his servants, was claimed by the Philistines; Isaac called it "Sitnah" ("hatred") and patiently surrendered it to avoid a conflict. A third well he named "Rehoboth" ("room"), for it was left unmolested in his control. God gave him a message of cheer, and a new promise of blessing, and he returned to his old home in Beer-sheba.

There he received a visit from Abimelech and other Philistine rulers, who implored Isaac to make with them a solemn covenant of peace. As a new well is dug there, it was called Beer-sheba, "the well of the oath."

In these dealings with the Philistines Isaac revealed what was possibly the most important trait of his character. This was his meekness. He was a man of peace. Meekness is not weakness, although the two are sometimes confused. Meekness does not demand any sentimental concession to injustice, any cowardly sacrifice of principle, any action which is contrary to conscience, or any surrender of the rights of others. It does not mean appeasement or "peace at any price." It does denote generosity, forbearance, humility, patience, long-suffering. It is the spirit which the apostle describes as "the meekness and gentleness of Christ." It is the rare virtue which should be cultivated more continually by the followers of the Prince of Peace.

Over the later years of Isaac there rest shadows of domestic discord. An old man, with failing sight, feeble, and too far dependent on the "creature comforts" provided by his favorite son, he determines to bestow on Esau the blessing which was understood to insure to its recipient the benefits promised to Abraham and his heirs. This purpose is foiled by the quick-witted Rebekah and their unscrupulous son Jacob. Disguised, and impersonating Esau, it proves possible for Jacob to secure from Isaac the coveted blessing. It is to the credit of Isaac that when the fraud is discovered he makes no complaint, and declares that the blessing cannot be recalled, and bestows on Esau a less glorious benediction. He probably remembers the divine intimation concerning these two brothers, "The elder shall serve the younger" (Ch. 25:23). However, his repentance is shown further. When Jacob is about to flee from the home, to escape the murderous resolve of Esau, the blessing is repeated with new emphasis: "God Almighty bless thee, and make thee fruitful, and multiply thee . . . and give thee the blessing of Abraham, to thee, and to thy seed with thee" (Ch. 28:3, 4).

However faulty the course of Isaac had been, it indicated his unfaltering confidence in the promises of God, which culminated in the assurance of the coming of One in whom all nations would be blessed. It should be noted that of all the incidents in the life of Isaac this one is selected in the New Testament as the supreme indication of his relation to God: "By faith Isaac blessed Jacob and Esau concerning things to come" (Heb. 11:20).

Evidently he forgave Jacob for his deception, for it was in the company and care of Jacob that he spent his closing days. Evidently, too, Jacob and Esau were reconciled, for in the closing scene, at the cave of Machpelah, both sons were present. When Isaac "gave up the ghost and died, and was gathered unto his people, being old and full of days, his sons Esau and Jacob buried him" (Ch. 35:29).

His character was in no sense colossal, as was that of his father Abraham, nor was his career colorful, as that of his son Jacob. Yet in his character there was much that was lovely and attractive. He was gentle, sympathetic, thoughtful, sensitive, humble, trustful. He appeals to our affection rather than to our admiration. During his long life, unlike other patriarchs, he was devoted to his one beloved wife. He was a worshiper of the true and living God. He is worthy of the place assigned him on the "honor roll of the heroes of faith" (Heb. 11:20).

# VI

# JACOB

GENESIS 25:19 TO 50:13

"AND JACOB WAS LEFT ALONE; AND THERE WRESTLED a man with him until the breaking of the day" (Ch. 32:24). *"Jacob was left alone."* It was a time of crisis in his life, and times of crisis usually are times of loneliness. There is the loneliness of an irreparable loss, or the loneliness of a secret sorrow, or of an irrevocable decision, or of a bitter moral struggle. It was the supreme crisis in the life of the patriarch. He then ceased to be Jacob; he became Israel, "a prince of God." *"And there wrestled a man with him."* This is rather more accurate than to say that he wrestled with a man. He had no thought of wrestling as that night he stood by the brook Jabbok. Out of the darkness a hand laid hold on him and held him in its powerful grasp. He indeed did struggle, until he was reduced to absolute helplessness and begged a blessing from his antagonist.

"There wrestled a man with him *until the breaking of day,*" until, in truth, a new day had dawned, until a new light had broken on his soul, until he learned the great lesson that *blessing comes only to confessed weakness in conscious dependence on God.*

That was a difficult lesson for Jacob to learn. It

97

came as the climax of long years of bitter *discipline*. He was by nature a man of strong will, ambitious, self-reliant, shrewd, resourceful, ready to resort to subtlety or craft. He was determined to succeed, by fair means if possible, by foul means if necessary; but succeed he must.

Yet there was much that was admirable in his character. He probably was deserving of less contempt than his brother Esau, with whom he often has been contrasted unfavorably. Esau is pictured commonly as the brave, generous, heroic, skillful hunter, and Jacob as the weak, unattractive, spoiled favorite of his mother. The fact seems to be that while Esau had broken away from the quiet pastoral life of his family and enjoyed a wild, reckless, self-indulgent career of pleasure and excitement, Jacob was a man of steady, moral, domestic habits, who stayed at home caring for the flocks and herds in which the wealth of the family consisted.

The essential difference between these two men lies deeper still. Jacob was a man of faith. He believed the promises which God had made to Abraham and Isaac, and that through him these promises were to be fulfilled; but his faith was imperfect. He supposed that in order to fulfill His purposes God needed not only the help but the trickery, the craftiness, the deceit of Jacob. Esau, on the other hand, was "profane" and worldly. To him the promises of future spiritual blessings seemed vague and unreal. They had little meaning or value. He lived for the enjoyment of the present, of the physical and sensual. It would seem that the parents encouraged the natural bent of their two sons. "Isaac loved Esau," not because of any nobility in his character, but "because he did eat of his venison, but Rebekah loved Jacob," not only because he remained in the home and cared for the family wealth, but because, before his birth, she had been assured that in him, her younger son, the divine purposes were to be fulfilled.

It had been predicted that "the elder" should "serve the younger"; but the birthright naturally belonged to Esau, the first-born. This birthright seems to have included the first place in the family, a double portion of the patrimony, and the inheritance of the promises made to Abraham. This birthright also needed to be confirmed by the blessing and benediction of Isaac. Therefore, if the prediction of primacy was to be fulfilled, Jacob, in some way, must secure the birthright and the blessing.

Years were passing. God seemed to have forgotten His purpose. Nothing was being done. So Jacob and Rebekah take matters into their own hands. Jacob is the first to act. He takes a mean advantage of his brother when an occasion offers. Esau has returned from the chase, famished with hunger. Jacob is cooking a mess of red lentils. "And Esau said to Jacob, Feed me, I pray thee, with that same red pottage, for I am faint. And Jacob said, Sell me this day thy birthright. And Esau said, Behold I am at the point to die, and what profit shall this birthright do to me? And Jacob said, Swear to me this day: and he sware unto him: and he sold his birthright unto Jacob. Then Jacob gave Esau bread and pottage of lentils; and he did eat and drink, and rose up, and went his way: thus Esau despised his birthright" (Ch. 25:29-34).

On the part of Jacob the bargain was cruel and faithless. Even if he believed the birthright was divinely promised, and so was his by right, he was guilty of that wrong rule of conduct which has darkened human history even to the present day; for he acted on the principle that "the end justifies the means," and that one is innocent if "doing evil that good may come."

On the other hand, the folly of Esau is even more pitiful. Through all the centuries the bargain he made has become proverbial for frivolity, weakness, madness, and senseless passion.

The birthright had been purchased, but it was quite as necessary to have it confirmed by the blessing and benediction of Isaac. Many years have passed. Isaac fears that his end is near. He determines to bestow on Esau the coveted blessing. He summons his son and bids him first secure for him some of his "savory venison," as though the gratification of his physical appetite might clarify his spiritual vision.

Now Rebekah steps on the scene, prompt, clever, resourceful. She instructs Jacob how to impersonate Esau and so secure the blessing in the absence of his brother. Jacob is an apt, if a somewhat timid, pupil. He is disguised as Esau; at first he feigns the part; then he lies, then he invokes the divine name and so is guilty of perjury; but the blessing is secured.

Success has been attained. Has it been attained? When Esau learns the truth he determines to kill Jacob. Then Rebekah advises Jacob to flee from the

murderous hate of his brother and to seek refuge in
the distant East, in the home of her brother Laban,
where he may obtain a wife. This last consideration
satisfies Isaac as he dismisses Jacob with a further
blessing.

Yet, has Jacob succeeded? Does he hold the chief
place in the family and does he possess a double portion of its wealth? The first night of his journey he
lies down to sleep, a failure, a fugitive, with no possession but his garments and his staff, with no shelter
under the cheerless sky, with only a stone for a pillow. Yet, in his sleep he has an arresting vision. He
dreams that he sees a ladder set up on earth and
reaching to heaven. On the ladder angels are ascend-
ing and descending, "and, behold, the Lord stood
above it, and said, I am the Lord God of Abraham
thy father, and the God of Isaac: the land whereon
thou liest, to thee will I give it, and to thy seed; . . .
and in thee and in thy seed shall all the families of
the earth be blessed. And, behold, I am with thee,
and will keep thee in all places whither thou goest,
and will bring thee again to this land" (Ch. 28:13-15).

This vision brought Jacob to a turning point in his
career. It has been called his "conversion." It was
then he realized, as never before, the presence, the
pardon, and the protecting care of the Lord. The poor
discouraged, defeated, remorseful man, borne down
by the sense of failure and chagrin, rises up to begin
life anew.

"Jacob awaked out of his sleep, and he said, Surely
the Lord is in this place; and I knew it not." In
reverential awe he exclaims, "How dreadful is this

place! this is none other but the house of God, and
this is the gate of heaven" (Ch. 28:16, 17).

This discovery of the presence and the grace of
God prompts an immediate act of worship. He "rose
up in the morning and took the stone that he had put
for his pillow, and set it up for a pillar, and poured
oil upon the top of it. And he called the name of that
place Bethel [that is, the "House of God"]" (Ch.
28:18, 19).

In this place of worship Jacob also makes a vow: "If
God will be with me, and will keep me in this way
that I go, and will give me bread to eat and raiment
to put on, so that I come again to my father's house
in peace; then shall the Lord be my God, and this
stone shall be God's house; and of all that thou shalt
give me I will surely give a tenth unto thee" (Ch.
28:20-22).

Jacob has been criticized for the form of this vow.
It is said that this was not an act of consecration but
an attempt to drive a bargain with the Lord. He
promises fidelity only on the condition of personal
benefit. This view is hardly fair to even such a crafty
character as Jacob. He asks nothing of the Lord. He
believes what God graciously has promised and in
return he makes his vow of consecration. His "if" is
probably "since." "Since God is to be with me, and
is to supply my need, and to bring me home in peace,
I pledge to him my obedience and trust, my worship
and adoration, and of all my wealth I shall bestow
upon him a tenth for his service."

It seems best to interpret this scene of Jacob at
Bethel as the picture of a man, who, disheartened by

failure in the past, by loneliness in the present, by fear of the future, is granted a vision of the grace of God. He yields himself to do the will of God, he chooses a place for the worship of God, and promises to devote his substance to the work of God.

Twenty full years elapse between this vision at Bethel and the night in which Jacob wrestles with the angel at the brook Jabbok. They are years of bitter discipline. Jacob is living with his "uncle" Laban, and a more trying experience it would be difficult to imagine, for of all the characters sketched in the Old Testament narrative, probably none is more contemptible than that of the pious fraud, the self-righteous trickster, Laban.

As will be remembered, Jacob makes his long and lonely journey across the desert. He reaches the city of Haran. At the well, outside the city, among the first persons he meets is his charming cousin Rachel. We read the interesting statement of the historian that "Jacob kissed Rachel and lifted up his voice and wept." It is well to conclude that his were tears of joy and emotion. Certainly it was a case of "love at first sight." Jacob gladly agrees to serve Laban, without wages, for seven years, if he then can claim Rachel as his wife. With all fidelity, and with real trust in God, he fulfills his promise: but when he claims his bride, he wakes up to find that Laban has palmed off on him poor, blear-eyed Leah, her elder sister.

When Laban makes the wretched excuse that it is not the custom of his country to give the younger in marriage before the elder, Jacob agrees to seven more years of service, and then finds that he has the best thing in the world, namely, the woman of his choice, but not enough wealth to support her. He has served fourteen years faithfully without recompense. He now makes an agreement with Laban for wages; but when he begins to acquire property, Laban changes the terms of the contract. This he does again and again, until, finally, the old disposition is awakened within Jacob. He has been patiently trusting the Lord. Now he takes matters into his own hands. It is now "diamond cut diamond" and "thief catch a thief"; and when an unscrupulous Jacob is matched with an unreliable Laban it is always Jacob who wins in the contest of wiles and wit.

An agreement is reached that, in caring for the flocks and herds, Jacob is to keep all the animals of abnormal color, the others to belong to Laban. However, by trickery and shrewdness, Jacob begins to grow immensely wealthy. The sons of Laban report to their father that their property is being lost. Trouble is brewing. A divine intimation comes to Jacob that it would be wise for him to leave Laban and to return to the land of promise.

He flees with his wives and children, his cattle and his goods, starting for the land of Canaan. Laban follows in hot pursuit, and after seven days he overtakes the caravan in Mount Gilead. Here Jacob adopts the familiar and usually successful ruse of claiming that he is the aggrieved party, and of accusing Laban of injustice before Laban can present his charges. Jacob is wholly successful, and a covenant is made between the two rivals. Beside a heap of stones they take a solemn vow that neither would pass that boundary

line to injure the other. They called the place
"*Mizpah*," for Laban said, "The Lord watch between
thee and me when we are absent one from another."
This is to say: "If either of us plans any action which
would break this agreement, may the Lord see to it
that the covenant is kept."

Thus Jacob again has triumphed by his own wit
and shrewdness. As a man of great wealth he is about
to enter the land of his boyhood and his dreams. So
he reaches the brook Jabbok.

He is self-confident as he faces the future. On his
way he has been met by a vision of angels, which
appeared to be a promise of the protection of God.
Yet, soon after, messengers arrived with the terrifying
news that Esau was coming to meet him with four
hundred men. This means peril, disaster, possibly
death, for he remembers the murderous hate of the
brother whom he had wronged.

However, he is always prompt to act. He divides all
his family and his possessions into two bands. It is a
clever compromise, for he said, "If Esau come to the
one company and smite it, then the other company
which is left will escape."

Then he prays. It is a humble, penitent prayer for
protection, pleading the promises of God. Then again
he acts. He forms a shrewd plan of appeasing his
brother with a rich bribe. He selects five hundred
and fifty of his choicest cattle, sheep, and camels, and
sends them across the Jabbok in nine separate droves,
with great spaces between, to make the greatest im-
pression with the least expense. With each drove goes
a servant, who is instructed to say, "These be thy

servant Jacob's: it is a present sent unto my lord Esau; and behold also he is behind us." This all may seem only Oriental courtesy; but it is rather suspicious on the part of the man who has secured Esau's birthright and blessing and is in reality the lord of Esau. Such, however, was his plan, "For he said, I will appease him with the present that goeth before me; . . . peradventure he will accept me."

He has done all that his cleverness and craft can suggest. In the night he sends his family and his flocks across the brook. "And Jacob was left alone." What will the next day bring? Is he at last to suffer for the trickery and deceit of the past years? As he reasons with himself he becomes more confident. He has always won. He will win again. He starts boldly to cross the stream. Then it is that in the darkness he is seized by a mysterious antagonist. He uses all his strategy and strength; but he wrestles in vain. At last he has met one whose power and skill are far beyond his own. He struggles until morning is streaking the eastern sky. Then his conqueror stretches out his hand and lays a finger on Jacob's thigh, and Jacob, defeated and subdued, hangs helpless on the neck of his divine adversary.

To the command, "Let me go," Jacob replies, "I will not let thee go, except thou bless me." The answer is significant: "What is thy name?" for there always must be confession before a blessing can be received. "And he said, Jacob," a trickster, a supplanter, a self-confident schemer. Then came the reply: "Thy name shalt be called no more Jacob, but Israel" (a prince of God). "And Jacob asked him, and said, Tell me, I pray thee, thy name," for a for-given penitent naturally wishes to know more of the grace and power of God. In answer to that prayer, "He blessed him there. And Jacob called the name of the place Peniel: for I have seen God face to face, and my life is preserved."

This experience at the Jabbok began a new epoch in the history of Jacob. He had learned the lesson that blessing comes, not by deceit and treachery, or even by self-confident effort, but by submission to God and dependence on His grace.

The character of Jacob has not been made perfect by the years of discipline or by that night of wrestling, but he is worthy now of his new name, "Israel," the "Prince." His character is further purified by the ex-periences of the following years. These were years of sunshine and shadow, of storm and calm. The discipline had not ended. There was much of sorrow, loss, trial, and anxiety to be endured. It is not only our happiness but our perfection that God seeks. Not by prosperity alone but also by adversity He purifies the character and consecrates it to His purposes.

Jacob crosses the Jabbok and meets Esau with humility and servile fear, but is greeted with generous affection. The reconciliation of the two brothers is apparently sincere and complete.

Jacob declines the offer of Esau to accompany him or to provide an armed escort. As Esau returns to his home in Seir, Jacob tarries for a time in the rich pasture of Succoth. He then crosses the Jordan. Here in the Land of Promise, at Shalem, a city of Shechem, he purchases a portion of land and erects an altar.

This altar is dedicated, not to the God of Abraham and Isaac; but is called El-elohe-Israel, "God, the God of Israel." This God, Jacob declares, is his God.

Such a personal, sustaining, guiding God, Jacob sorely needs. Because of the savage and treacherous revenge taken by his sons on the men of Shechem, Jacob is compelled to withdraw from the land.

Under divine guidance he reaches Bethel. Here it was that years ago, when fleeing from his angry brother, he had received a vision and had vowed his consecration to God. Now he puts away all idolatry from among his followers, erects another altar, and receives from God a new assurance that his descendants will become "a company of nations," and will be given the land of Canaan.

At Bethel, "Deborah Rebekah's nurse died." The respectful sorrow shown by Jacob for this aged servant of the household reflects credit upon his character. However, a greater sorrow awaits him. As he journeys southward and nears Ephrath (Bethlehem), he is crushed by the sudden loss of his fondly cherished wife. Rachel dies soon after giving birth to her second son, Benjamin. She has been the joy of Jacob's life, the very idol of his heart. His passionate devotion to her may account for the favoritism shown to her two sons. Probably, too, they had inherited something of their mother's grace and charm, which contrasted with the crude and gross character of their brothers.

As Jacob reaches Hebron, which for many years is to be his home, he has the comfort of a reunion with his aged father Isaac and the satisfaction of caring for his declining days, and also the melancholy privilege

of attending with Esau his burial in the cave of
Machpelah.

The partiality of Jacob for the sons of Rachel was
marked particularly in his treatment of Joseph. It
explains, in part, why his brothers so envied him, and
hated him, and, when opportunity offered, sold him as
a slave into Egypt. Furthermore, it explains why
Jacob, when the necessity arose, so long refused to
allow Benjamin to accompany his brothers when they
returned to the mysterious ruler in the court of
Pharaoh.

Those had been long and lonely years since Jacob
had been deprived of the companionship of Joseph;
he could not face the possible loss of the other son
of his beloved Rachel.

It would be impossible to imagine the bewildered
surprise and joy felt by the aged patriarch when he
learns that Joseph is alive, that he is prime minister
of Egypt, and that he has invited his father to join
him at the command of the king.

If Jacob felt any hesitation in accepting the invita-
tion of Pharaoh to leave the Land of Promise, it was
removed, when, passing southward he paused at Beer-
sheba to worship. There, in a night vision, he received
a divine message: "I am God, the God of thy father:
fear not to go down into Egypt, for I will there make
of thee a great nation. I will go down with thee into
Egypt; and I will also surely bring thee up again:
and Joseph shall put his hand upon thine eyes" (Ch.
46:3, 4).

Those last years, spent in Egypt, were like a radiant
but peaceful sunset at the close of a day of storm and

tempest. Jacob was honored by the king, surrounded by his sons, and dwelt amidst the plenty of the fertile land of Goshen. His eyes grew dim, but his spiritual sight seemed to grow more bright as he summoned his sons and bestowed on them his parting blessing. Indeed, the faith of Jacob is revealed less in any other scene of his eventful career than in the closing chapter, when he looks into the distant future with unquestioning faith in the promises of God.

As we read those last pages in the life of the aged prince whom Pharaoh delighted to honor, as we dwell on the picture of that royal cortege which finally escorted the embalmed body from Egypt to the tomb of his ancestors in Hebron, we are less impressed than by the predictions made by the dying patriarch as he looked with inspired vision into the future which God had revealed. From all the incidents in his life, the author of Hebrews, wishing to record the message of his career, relates only this one: "By faith Jacob blessed both the sons of Joseph" (Heb. 11:21). That blessing of his grandsons came first; and with surprising discrimination, even against the protest of Joseph, the chief blessing was given, not to the elder Manasseh, but to the younger son Ephraim.

Then, one by one, his twelve sons passed before him. One by one he touched on their past, and one by one he predicted their future. The whole address is an idyllic and prophetic poem. Reuben, Simeon, and Levi have forfeited the favor and the blessing of their father. Other sons are mentioned in brief but significant phrases. It is on Judah that the chief benediction rests. The aged patriarch, who never doubted the blessing certain to come to all nations through his descendants, seems to concentrate his prophetic gaze on One, a Prince of the tribe of Judah. We well may believe that this spirit, purified and enobled by divine discipline, catches a vision, dim but glorious, as he is heard to say:

> The scepter shall not depart from Judah,
>   Nor a lawgiver from between his feet,
> Until Shiloh come;
>   And to him shall be the obedience of the peoples.
> (Ch. 49:10).

# VII

## *JOSEPH*

THE STORY OF JOSEPH, THE PURE AND PRINCELY PRIME
minister of Egypt, possesses an unfailing fascination
and charm. Because of its dramatic movement, its
brilliant color, its play of all the elemental passions,
and its abiding human interest, it is quite commonly
regarded as without a peer among the short stories of
the world. Its supreme importance lies in the fact that
it shows how the family of patriarchs could develop
into a great race; it prepares us for the history of the
birth of a nation. While in Canaan, the children of
Israel could not have grown and expanded, as only
contracted places of sojourn were grudgingly granted
them by surrounding tribes. They needed to be
brought down to Egypt, where they could regard as
their own the spacious and fertile land of Goshen.

This story is significant further as it explains how,
when finally enslaved by the Egyptians, the race, even
under the conditions of cruel and bitter bondage,
could so multiply as to become a formidable and
enviable power. The explanation is found in the
influence of Joseph, whose principles and character
were cherished and imitated as those of the greatest

and most revered of national heroes. In his own life
the molding influence had been his faith in God. This
was the secret of his prophetic visions, of his notable
victories, and of his conspicuous career.

## THE VISIONS OF FAITH

The dreams of Joseph are the index to the story.
As the chorus of a Greek tragedy or a prologue in a
Shakespearean play, they outline and make clear the
plot of the drama. Some readers have criticized Joseph
for narrating his dreams; they regard this as revealing
the one weakness in his character and as the needless
cause of all his severe trials. This is to miss the literary
artistry and real meaning of the narrative. Here is a
plot in which dreams are determining factors. Joseph's
conduct was inspired by his dreams; the interpretation
of dreams resulted in his deliverance from prison, and
later placed him next to the throne. However naive
or even self-conscious he may appear as he relates his
dreams to his brothers and his father, this was not
a sign of childish vanity or pride; it was an exhibition
of faith. Joseph regarded his visions as the veritable
voice of God.

He saw his sheaf standing upright while the sheaves
of his brothers bowed before it; he saw the sun and
moon and the eleven stars making obeisance to him.
His brothers and his father naturally interpreted the
dreams as implying his superiority to them. He saw
in these symbols a divine promise of a lofty destiny,
of distinguished and exalted position and power.

There is always a natural or psychological basis for a

dream. The elements have been in the mind before. In fact, nothing can be in the field of imagination which has not been previously in the field of consciousness. The elements may be combined fantastically, absurdly, but they have been seen before. No other person could dream your dreams.

So Joseph's dreams were composed of factors which his father had placed in his mind. He was known as as the elder son of a mother whom Jacob adored. He was to hold the chief place in the household, and probably for this reason had been given as a badge of distinction and superiority a "robe of many colors," or a "long cloak reaching to the ankles." He had been told of the glorious destiny of the family. What could be more natural than the dreams which he dreamed?

However, these were visions of faith. He believed they were not only messages but promises from God. This is a drama of dreams; but Joseph in prison declared his belief: "Do not interpretations belong to God?" and in the presence of the king he was heard to say of the strange dreams which had been related, "God hath shewed unto Pharaoh what he is about to do." In this belief Joseph rehearsed, and in this faith he cherished his own dreams. Through his darkest hours he was strengthened and sustained by them. In his princely exaltation he saw them fulfilled.

Let us cherish our dreams; not the fantastic visions of the night, but the high ideals inspired by our Christian faith, and the glorious promises of the Christian gospel. By them let us be strengthened and encouraged. Let us keep them bright before us and never allow them to fade into the light of common day.

## The Victories of Faith

The life of Joseph embodied a series of notable triumphs. *First of all*, was his victory over the temptation to despondency and despair. He was cast into a pit by his cruel brothers. This black cavern, dug in the desert as a reservoir for water, had a narrow opening at the top which was covered by a stone and could not be reached by a helpless prisoner because of high sloping walls. Delivered from this living death, Joseph is sold into Egypt as a slave. He who was to occupy the chief place in the family is thus torn from his home forever. He who was to enjoy an exalted career, is now in a position of hopeless degradation and shame. Yet he does not yield to bitter resentment or to morbid self-pity. Purchased by Potiphar, a prince who stands near Pharaoh, he proves to be so keenly alive to every possibility before him, so faithful to every duty, so capable in every position, that soon he is appointed as steward, in complete control of the estate of his master the Egyptian lord.

Then he is foully slandered and cast for life into a royal prison. Yet his courage never fails. He is the most cheerful and helpful and sympathetic and dependable of all those in confinement. His worth and ability are recognized by the keeper of the prison, who "committed to Joseph's hand all the prisoners that were in the prison; and whatsoever they did, he was the doer of it . . . because the Lord was with him and that which he did the Lord made it to prosper."

Before his imprisonment a *second victory* had been won. This was the triumph over the temptation to impurity. It had come in the seductive form of an Egyptian princess. The wife of Potiphar had been so attracted by the buoyant spirit, the charm, the youthful vigor of Joseph that she conceived a guilty passion for him. His trial was severe. To yield was safe. It was the way of possible advancement. To refuse was to face the mad hatred of a spurned and infuriated woman. How did Joseph win the victory? First, by remembering how much he owed to his master. Gratitude made him hesitate so to deceive and wrong one who had reposed in him unbounded trust. Sin is always selfish. One cannot do wrong without casting a shadow on some other life.

In the second place, Joseph realized that impurity is a defiance of God: "How then," replies Joseph, "can I do this wickedness, and sin against God?" It sometimes strengthens one to remember that God has established laws to insure our happiness and well-being; to break these laws is rebellion against the Ruler of a moral universe. The issue must be pain and loss.

In the third place, Joseph insisted on avoiding the temptation. Some modern novelists have missed or misstated this important fact. They have implied that Joseph courted the society of the temptress. The sacred narrative reaches its climax in the clear statement that he would not "be with her." It is wise to "flee from temptation." "Let him that thinketh he standeth take heed lest he fall." It has further been imagined that Joseph was kept from sin by a vision of his father's face. Whatever influence the memory of Jacob may have had, it was rather a vision of the face of God which sustained Joseph, and the recollection of those dreams of true greatness and power which had seemed to him the very voice of the Lord.

The *third victory* of Joseph was over the temptation to an abuse of power and to a life of self-indulgence and ease. Prosperity is often a severer test of character than adversity. When Joseph was taken from the dungeon and placed next to the throne he used all his powers for the good of the nation and in the service of the king. He interpreted the dreams of Pharaoh as predicting seven years of plenty to be followed by seven years of famine, and he advised the king to preserve all possible surplus in the years of plenty to be used in the years of want.

When appointed by the king to execute this wise plan, he exhibited three admirable qualities of a public servant. First, he established an economy of *thrift*, which provided for a surplus rather than of extravagance and waste and of public debt. Second, he was *diligent* in his task, which demanded careful organization and wise supervision of the vast resources of Egypt. Third, he showed marvelous *patience*. As for seven years there was no sign of famine, the counselors of the king may have derided one who was shaping the economy of a nation because of his interpretation of a dream. He may have been regarded as a visionary. However, his plans were very practical. For seven years he collected one-fifth of all the abundant harvests and stored the food in cities: "Joseph gathered corn as the sand of the sea, very much, until he left numbering: for it was without number" (Ch. 41:49).

Then came the years of famine. "And Joseph gath-

ered up all the money that was found in the land of
Egypt and in the land of Canaan for the corn which
they bought: and Joseph brought the money into
Pharaoh's house." When the money failed, Joseph
secured the cattle for Pharaoh. Then in exchange
for food Joseph bought all the land. Then the people
themselves became obligated to the king, and in exchange for seed they paid a twenty per cent income
tax on all that the fields produced. The people, however, were grateful and said: "thou hast saved our
lives, let us find grace in the sight of my lord and we
will be Pharaoh's servants."

We do not approve of such a monarchial form of
government, but it is impressive under any regime to
find a public servant who is wholly unselfish; and there
is for all of us a message, as we read of one who only
and ever sought to advance the interests of his king.
Surely the times demand such rulers, and for Christians there should be a determination to serve more
loyally our divine Ruler, our gracious King.

The supreme temptation of Joseph was not despondency, or impurity, or self-indulgence, but the
temptation to take *revenge*. Here he won his *supreme
victory*, and to this triumph a surprising portion of
the story is devoted. Joseph's treatment of his brothers
is the essential feature of this drama.

"When Jacob saw there was corn in Egypt" he sent
his sons, excepting Benjamin, to purchase food. They
appeared in the presence of Joseph, the prime minister
and food administrator, and "bowed down themselves
before him with their faces to the earth. . . . And
Joseph knew his brethren, but they knew not him. . . .

And Joseph remembered the dreams which he dreamed of them." Yes, but he remembered much more. He remembered the fierce envy aroused by those dreams. He remembered the pit into which they had cast him. He remembered his cries and entreaties and the brutal cruelty of those heartless men. Now the dream was fulfilled. Now they were prostrate before him. Now they were absolutely in his power. Now was the time to taste the sweetness of revenge. Should he select for them imprisonment, torture, or death? What did he do? He forgave them all. He revealed the princely quality of his nature. When, after long weeks of testing, he learned that they would understand and be better for his pardon, he said, "Be not grieved, nor angry with yourselves, that ye sold me hither; for God did send me before you to preserve life" (Ch. 45:5). He entertains them as royal guests. He brings to Egypt their aged father and presents him to the king. He receives for their residence the rich land of Goshen.

It was a victory of faith. He believed that God had overruled their cruelty for good. There is nothing more royal, more princely, more noble than the ability to forgive and to forget. "Be kind one to another," writes the Apostle Paul, "tender hearted forgiving one another even as God for Christ's sake hath forgiven you." It will help us to be forgiving if we remember what our pardon has cost. In Christ "we have redemption through his blood, the forgiveness of sins, according to the riches of his grace" (Eph. 1:7).

### The Vindication of Faith

The words of pardon spoken by Joseph to his brothers contain the supreme message of his life. He believed in the overruling power of God, who would make all things work together for good. This story of Joseph constitutes a romance of providence.

Is it wise always to trust and obey God? If one suffers and sacrifices for the sake of what is right, is there certain to be deliverance and recompense? Probably one should not ask such questions, but there are occasions on which they thrust themselves on the stricken soul with irresistible force. Could a loving God allow an innocent lad to be sold as a slave by his cruel brothers? Is it just to allow a faithful servant to be slandered and cast into a hopeless dungeon? All such questions find an answer in the story of Joseph. The mystery is not wholly solved, but here is exhibited an inspiring vindication of faith. Here it is found that the pit and the prison are stepping-stones to the scepter and the throne. Here again is an assurance that in time or in eternity one will have reason to praise the unfailing justice and mercy and providence of God.

Thus in this story it is not difficult to find a vindication of faith in God; but how can we vindicate Joseph? He did forgive his brothers; but first he submitted them to mental torture. How can one explain or excuse his apparent cruelty?

As soon as he recognizes them he casts them into a dungeon. One can imagine what it meant for these shepherds, who were accustomed to the great open

spaces, to be shut up in suffocation and darkness.
Then, at the command of Joseph, Simeon is left
bound in the prison house and the brothers are sent
back to Jacob with the command that they are not to
return to Egypt unless they bring with them Benjamin,
the beloved son of Jacob, who has been left at home.
On their journey they are mystified to find the purchase money in their sacks of grain.

Jacob is reluctant to allow Benjamin to leave him.
Yet, under pressure of the famine, he consents, and
now, on their arrival in Egypt, all the brothers are
ushered into the presence of Joseph. They are royally
received, and, after being fêted and banqueted, they
are sent back to Canaan. Hardly are they on their
way when they are overtaken by soldiers and accused
of having stolen a silver cup from Joseph. Vowing
their innocence, they declare "with whomsoever of
thy servants it be found, let him die and we also will
be my lord's bondmen." Imagine their anguish of
soul when "the cup was found in Benjamin's sack."
As they prostrate themselves before Joseph, Judah acts
as their spokeman. He confesses their guilt not only
in reference to the cup but in their former treatment
of Joseph, of whom the strange Egyptian prince is
supposed to be ignorant. This may be the fuller
meaning of the words, "God hath found out the
iniquity of thy servants." Judah speaks touchingly of
Jacob. If Benjamin fails to return, Jacob will die of
sorrow. Then, last of all, he offers, for the sake
of Jacob, to remain in Egypt and to suffer in the place
of his brother.

This noble speech is enough for Joseph. It is, indeed, more than he can endure. His purpose has been accomplished. No longer can he disguise his feelings. He weeps aloud. He sobs out his complete pardon: "I am Joseph. . . . God sent me before you to preserve you a posterity in the earth, and to save your lives by a great deliverance."

Why this long-delayed forgiveness? Why this painful process of trial? Joseph had waited until he could discover three things: first, had these brothers repented of their crime against him? He has found that the sorrow for their sin is sincere. He has heard them cry while ignorant of his identity: "We were verily guilty concerning our brother, in that we saw the anguish of his soul, when he besought us and we would not hear, therefore is this distress come upon us."

Second, how did they feel toward one another? In the days of Joseph's boyhood they were cruel, heartless, jealous, violent; now they are willing to die one for another.

Third, had they come to have real love for Jacob? Were they willing now to break his heart as when they showed him the blood-stained robe of Joseph, causing him to believe that his favorite son had been killed by a wild beast? Now their whole course was shaped by their tender sympathy for the aged patriarch. They were dismayed at the thought of returning to Jacob if they left Benjamin in Egypt: "It shall come to pass, when he seeth that the lad is not with us, that he will die: and thy servants shall bring down the gray hairs of thy servant our father with sorrow to the grave."

When Joseph knew of their penitence, when he

was sure that they sympathized one with another, when they showed their love for Jacob, then he could declare the pardon and the deep affection which until then he felt it necessary to conceal.

Here is a message for each one who would experience the pardoning grace of God. Has one repented of his sin? Does he feel sympathy for others? Is there in his heart real love for God? If so, the visions of faith will grow brighter, the victories of faith will be more continuous, and the vindication of faith will be complete when one is brought by his Elder Brother into the palace of the King.

In the case of Joseph, as he interprets the gracious providence of God, his thought extends far beyond the immediate circle of his own household. He shows his forgiveness by bringing to Egypt his father and his brothers, by presenting them to the king, and by securing for them a residence in the rich land of Goshen. He listens to Jacob as he pronounces his prophecies on each of his twelve sons. He buries his father with royal honors in the Land of Promise. Then, when his brothers fear that Joseph will at last take revenge, he renews his assurance of pardon, and looks out to the distant future and sees the generations, which, in the providence of God, are being affected through him. "And Joseph said unto them, Fear not: for am I in the place of God? But as for you, ye thought evil against me: but God meant it unto good, to bring to pass, as it is this day, to save much people alive."

How far the vision of Joseph extended we do not know. Surely he remembered the promises of universal blessing made to Abraham and Isaac and Jacob. Surely he recalled his own dreams. Whatever he may have meant by saving "much people alive," we know that the providence of God kept alive that family which developed into the race from which came the Saviour of the world.

Of this Saviour there is found in Joseph a worthy and a significant type. Each was a well-beloved son. Each was envied and hated by his brethren. Each was sold for a few pieces of silver. Both were given over to die. Both came forth to new life, one from a prison-house and One from a tomb. Both were given places of supreme power; one as prime minister of Pharaoh, the Other as "King of kings," now "seated at the right hand of God." Both proved to be Deliverers and Redeemers. One rescued the brothers by whom he had been hated and betrayed, the Other "is able to save unto the uttermost those that come unto God by him." Joseph looked across the centuries to a time when his people would be brought to Canaan, and with this in view he secured a pledge that his body should be laid to rest in the Land of Promise. Christ confidently predicted that the hour would come when His voice would call to life "all that are in the graves." He promised to return in power and great glory. Of that glory his brethren are to partake. Joseph is a veritable *symbol of sovereignty*, of the sovereignty which is to be exercised by Christ and shared by His followers (Rev. 3:21). His rule is the hope of the world. For His coming we are to watch and to wait, and so to live that we confidently can pray: "Even so, come, Lord Jesus." Amen.